D0275176

High Five!

OTHER BOOKS BY
KEN BLANCHARD AND SHELDON BOWLES:

Gung ho!

Raving Fans!

Big Bucks!

OTHER BOOKS BY KEN BLANCHARD

The One Minute Manager (with Spencer Johnson)

Putting the One Minute Manager to Work (with Robert Lorber)

Leadership and the One Minute Manager (with Patricia Zigarmi and Drea Zigarmi)

The One Minute Manager Builds High Performing Teams (with Donald Carew and Eunice Parisi-Carew)

The One Minute Sales Person (with Spencer Johnson)

The One Minute Manager Meets the Monkey (with William Oncken Jr and Hal Burrows)

High Five!

The Magic of Working Together

Ken Blanchard and *Sheldon Bowles*
with *Don Carew* and *Eunice Parisi-Carew*

HarperCollins*Business*
An Imprint of HarperCollins*Publishers*

HarperCollinsBusiness
An Imprint of HarperCollins*Publishers*
77–85 Fulham Palace Road,
Hammersmith, London W6 8JB

www.**fire**and**water**.com/business

Published by HarperCollinsBusiness 2001
1 3 5 7 9 8 6 4 2

First published in the USA by
William Morrow, an Imprint of HarperCollins Inc 2001

A catalogue record for this book
is available from the British Library

ISBN 0 00 710821 4

Printed and bound in Great Britain by
Clays Ltd, St Ives plc

Dedicated to

LARRY HUGHES

Editor, Mentor, Friend

The best teammate
an author
could ever ask for

FOREWORD

When Ken Blanchard asked me to write a foreword for *High Five!* I said I would be most honored to do so. After reading the manuscript, I'm especially honored. I love this book!

High Five! stimulated my mind, reminding me that any individual can achieve more if he or she is part of a good team—especially in these increasingly complex and changing times.

Even more important, the story touched my heart, as I hope it touches yours. It shows us how having a purpose beyond ourselves adds great meaning to our lives in a way that is inspiring and nourishing.

Ken not only knows about working as part of a team, he *lives* it. He is one of the best teammates I have ever had the enjoyment of working with.

When we wrote *The One Minute Manager* together, one plus one was much greater than two. We shared a common purpose: to communicate simple truths to people in an easy-to-understand way that would help them live more effective lives. We built upon each other's strengths and had fun in the process. We know the result has been greater than what either of us could have achieved alone.

We rekindled our team effort with the book *Who Moved My Cheese?* Without Ken's prodding and encouragement, I don't know if I would have ever written that book.

Now comes *High Five!* As soon as I finished reading it, I knew I was going to share it widely among my colleagues who are on the various teams I am a part of. Reading this story can motivate us all to be better team players and improve our results.

If we are to survive and thrive in the twenty-first century, learning to work successfully in teams is a must.

As Ken and his teammates, Sheldon Bowles, coauthor of *Raving Fans*, *Gung Ho!*, and *Big Bucks!*, and Don Carew and Eunice Parisi-Carew, long-term consulting partners in Ken and his wife Margie's training and consulting company and experts on team development, emphasize, "*None of us is as smart as all of us.*"

I hope you find what you are looking for in this readable and touching story and, when you do, that you raise your hand high in the air and give yourself and others on your team a great high five!

Spencer Johnson, M.D.,
author of *Who Moved My Cheese?* and coauthor of
The One Minute Manager

High Five!

PROLOGUE

Fired!

It burned in his brain.

His vice president was saying reengineering, downsizing, redundancy, and even "Nothing personal, Alan. No reflection on your work."

But Alan Foster knew that was garbage. He knew all the fancy words were garbage, too. Reengineering meant fired. Finished. Not wanted.

There would be a generous severance package and outplacement counseling, but Alan wasn't listening. His head was churning, trying to understand what was happening. Somewhere in the back of his mind he knew he wasn't fitting in the way he used to. He knew he'd been spoken to any number of times about it and he hadn't changed. But those were relationship issues. The way he worked with others. That wasn't something Alan could conceive of getting fired for!

He was escorted to his office and told to pack his personal belongings; twenty-one minutes later he stood beside his car with a cardboard box of family photos, books, pens, and two cans of diet soda from his bottom drawer.

"Good-bye, Mr. Foster," said the security guard who had escorted him out and helped by carrying the framed painting he and Susan had bought two years before.

The guard stepped back, hesitated, and then said, "Sorry to see you go. You always treated me well."

"Damn right," thought Alan as he placed the box and picture into the backseat of his car. "I treated everyone well."

As if to confirm his words, and mock him at the same time, Alan's eyes fell on an engraved plaque, sitting in the box, presented to him five years earlier: The Production Excellence Award.

That's what hurt. He may not have been a superstar, but he was a good producer. When he was given a personal goal, he met it. His reports were always on time. He was never over budget. He was in compliance 100 percent with every policy and procedure. He even personally—yes, personally—took the seven ladies in the secretarial pool to lunch on Valentine's Day.

He slammed closed the back door of his Ford. Known for keeping a cool head when trouble struck, Alan was surprised to find himself getting angry. He'd given this company ten good years, and now he'd been tossed aside on the reengineering dump of the no longer needed.

He was about to get into his car when he saw the company's new president, George Burton, parking his gray Cadillac ten spaces down from what, until now, had been Alan's space. Mr. Burton had been there six months. Yet he remained while Alan, after ten years, was being tossed out.

Hardly realizing what he was doing, Alan walked over and confronted Mr. Burton as he got out of his car.

"I just got fired," Alan announced in a voice that made both his frustration and anger evident.

"Yes. I know," said Mr. Burton.

"But I'm a good producer," Alan said as his frustration overcame his anger.

"You are," agreed Mr. Burton.

"Then why?" pleaded Alan. "I don't understand."

Mr. Burton looked as if he was about to give Alan the reengineering and downsizing speech, but after a slight hesitation he reached out, put a hand on Alan's shoulder, looked him directly in the eye, and in a firm but kind voice delivered the honest truth: "Personal production isn't the issue. The issue is, you're not a team player, Alan. I need good producers, yes, but I need good producers who are team players, too."

Alan was going to protest when Mr. Burton added, "Think about it, Alan. You do great on your own, but the rest of your team isn't doing very well. You're a puck hog, Alan. You're a one-man hockey team, and that can't work today. I need people who can work together for our goals. Sure, you'd score less, but the team would score a whole lot more. As president, I have to be concerned with maximizing the contributions of everyone. Fact is, Alan, you're costing us money."

With that Mr. Burton said, "Good luck, Alan," pulled his briefcase off the front seat, and with what might have been an apologetic smile, turned and left Alan standing there, alone and unemployed.

Alan walked slowly back to his car and drove home.

Susan was a saint.

"Don't worry, dear. You're good. You'll get another job easily. And a better job, too!"

Alan figured he could get another job all right. But a better job? He wasn't so sure. He knew Mr. Burton was right. He wasn't a team player. Alan didn't mean to hog the puck the way Mr. Burton accused. It was just that for him puck passing and scoring goals didn't go together. They never had.

Since leaving home at sixteen he'd been his own man. The Air Force had given him his formal education and taught him to fly. Crew loved to fly with Alan. Other pilots might walk a perfunctory check around their aircraft before takeoff. Alan inspected everything. It was ironic. The crew trusted him because he trusted no one. He even checked the sophisticated military weather forecasts with civilian ones.

Later, as a businessman, Alan continued life as a one-man band. He kept control of everything. With high energy, hard work, and a sharp mind he always exceeded his goals, even if the team didn't. His boss had told him many times that he had to become a team player. He'd try but would quickly revert to his old ways. They produced results—at least for Alan they did.

But Alan could sense the world was changing. In every industry it was the team players who were in demand. The days of a lone wolf like Alan, good producer or not, were ending. And while Alan didn't know it, even if he had been a superstar, at least what he'd have called a superstar, that wouldn't have saved him. His definition of superstar and George Burton's definition were very different. A superstar to George Burton had to meet two tests: personal production and, equally important, a superstar had to make the rest of his or her team more productive; way more productive. Alan's idea of superstar didn't go beyond the first test.

CHAPTER 1

Loud, constant cheers and the crack of wooden hockey sticks frantically trying to get the puck rang out in the frigid air and bounced back from the arena's concrete walls and the wooden stands where parents were stamping their feet to keep warm.

On the ice there was a mad scramble behind the home net as the clock hit zero, the horn sounded, and the game ended. The spectators quickly exited to the heated canteen while the players headed for the dressing rooms.

When it came to energy, drive, and enthusiasm, the grade-five boys hockey team at Riverbend Elementary School was truly remarkable. Every single player was destined for NHL stardom.

At least that's what they believed. If unflinching belief in one's own ability and a can-do attitude were the magic key to success, the Riverbend Warriors would have been at the top of their league.

Unfortunately, in reality, they had lost most of their games. When they won, it usually meant the opposing team was playing even worse hockey. And this Saturday, Riverbend had lost again.

As Alan Foster watched his son, David, and his teammates go down to yet another humiliating loss, he marveled at how little the boys seemed aware of their own shortcomings. Skating off the ice they were defiant in defeat. A bad referee, bad ice, bad breaks, and even bad skate sharpening were among the culprits being named. No one was accepting responsibility, individually or collectively, for the loss.

"Another great night of grade-five hockey," said Alan to Coach Milt Gorman while David, down in the locker room, changed to street clothes.

"I've always dreamed of a great team. Instead, once again we got our heads handed to us," replied Milt with a warm laugh.

"You and Coach Nanton really are wonderful the way you give so much time to this," said Alan.

"Gives me a chance to spend time with my son, and besides, I love the game," said Coach Gorman as he stepped out of the player's box on his way to the locker room. "Some days, though, I do wish I didn't have a team with half of the boys frightened to go after the puck and the other half hogging the puck the second they get their stick on it."

The reference to puck hogs rattled Alan, but not as much as Coach Gorman's next words: "David told my Billy that you got cut loose at work."

"That's right," replied Alan with more brusqueness than he intended.

"Sorry to hear that," said Milt as he swung several spare hockey sticks up on his shoulder. "Bad luck."

"No," Alan heard himself saying emphatically, "not bad luck. The last four or five years the company has been changing. I didn't. The result was I didn't fit anymore. It wasn't bad luck or even a bad ref or bad ice. It was my fault."

"Jeez," said Milt. "If our kids had half the guts and gumption you've got to take personal responsibility for what happens, they might really be on their way to the NHL."

"To tell the truth, this is the first time I've admitted it to myself or anyone else," said Alan. "I guess listening to those kids leaving the ice with all their misplaced grumbling was a wake-up call."

Alan's admission was also right in line with his one-man-band philosophy. He believed he had only himself to count on, so no one else could take the blame. It also provided a way to avoid facing the real problem. He had accepted responsibility. What more could he do? Case closed. No need to look deeper or further.

Of course, Milt wasn't aware of this. He was thinking about something entirely different.

"Well, here's the thing," said Milt. "I really didn't mean to embarrass you."

"No problem," said Alan.

"Nice of you to say. But what I was trying to get at is that Gus Nanton and I could really use help with these kids. I know from David that work used to keep you busy most evenings and weekends, but I was hoping you might have the time now to give us a hand."

"Me teach hockey? I haven't skated in years. I'm not even sure I remember the rules," said Alan.

"I know the rules. Coach Nanton skates beautifully. Besides, as coaches we have only one job and that's to get these kids working as a team, teaching them that everyone, working together, will accomplish more than each of them giving 100 percent individually. That's where we could use some help. If these kids learn the magic of teamwork, we'll have given them a greater gift than all the skating practice and rule drill ever could."

The arena, which minutes before had reverberated with the clash of sticks and cheers, was now deserted except for Alan and Milt.

"Okay," said Alan, taking a deep breath. "Second honest confession of the night. The change I got fired over? Teamwork. I got fired even though I was one of their best producers because I wasn't a team player. I'd hardly be the one to teach teamwork."

Milt cocked his head to the side as if to better consider what Alan had said. Then, shifting the weight of the hockey sticks on his shoulder, he replied: "That company may not want you, but I do. I think you'll be perfect. You don't have to sing like Pavarotti to teach singing."

Actually, Milt wasn't really concerned with perfection or even being average. He just needed another parent to share the load.

Sensing interest, Milt continued: "My wife and I sell bottled water from our store for a living. Gus Nanton is a graphic designer—on his own, works out of his basement office. We know nothing about teamwork. At least you know something about it. Around here," he added with a laugh, "you'll be our expert!"

Then Milt Gorman said the words Alan needed to hear more than anything. Slowly, deliberately, and sincerely he said, "I want you, Alan."

"I'd love to do it," Alan said softly to keep his voice from cracking with gratitude. He was wanted.

"Practice at seven p.m. Tuesday then?" said Milt.

"Sure thing," replied Alan.

"That's great; and thanks. I'm looking forward to working with you," Milt called back as he disappeared down the ramp to the dressing room.

Alan's explanation to his wife began simply: "You've heard that saying, people teach what they most need to learn themselves? Well, I'm going to be teaching teamwork to the Riverbend Warriors."

Teaching, not learning, however, was Alan's aim. Teamwork was fine for a sport like hockey or basketball, but in Alan's world, the world he thought of as the real world, if you wanted to get something done, you did it yourself. When Alan's butt was on the proverbial line, Alan trusted no one but himself to cover it. The fact that being a lone wolf had cost him his job, while working with his team would have saved him, was an irony lost on Alan.

At Milt's house later that evening, his wife, Anna, turned out her bedside light, snuggled up against her husband, and said, "So he gets fired because he is such an awful team player, and you take him on to teach teamwork?"

"That's it," Milt admitted.

"If I ever forget why I love you, just remind me of this, please. You're wonderful," Anna replied.

CHAPTER 2

Alan Foster began his coaching career in the sports section of the public library, and in the shelves with books on "team building" and "teamwork."

His real education, though, was on Tuesday and Thursday nights when the Riverbend Warriors practiced and on Saturday evening when seventeen grade-five hockey stars suited up, took to the ice, and three weeks out of four went down to defeat.

During practice they tried to teach the boys three things. First of all, skills. They drilled skating down the ice at full speed. When Coach Nanton blew his whistle, that was the signal to screech to a stop, turn, and power-skate back up the ice until the whistle blew again. At least that was the theory. Screeching to a stop generally meant gliding to a halt for the worst skaters; sliding into a slow sweeping turn for most. Only one or two would attempt to brake with the side of their skate blade, often falling down in the process. They also drilled on passing, puck handling, and fast slap shots on goal. Again, that was the theory. Reality was different. Aside from one player, Jed Boothe, who was blessed with some natural talent and coordination, skills seemed almost nonexistent.

Second came sportsmanlike conduct, the rules of the game and traditions. One tradition no longer taught at the grade-five level was lining up at center ice after the game and skating past the opposing team to shake hands.

"Too many fights were breaking out, so the league governors took the easy way and canceled the skate-past instead of clamping down on the troublemakers and the coaches who allowed it," Milt told Alan with evident disgust during Alan's first practice session with the kids.

"Weak-kneed, weak-willed, weak-minded do-gooders, who spend their time in meetings rather than actually out on the ice with the kids, are taking over and ruining this game. They're teaching a whole generation that barnyard bullies are really in control!"

The third area of teaching, the one where Milt said they had the best chance to combat the bad example and messages of the league governors, was teamwork: learning how to set up a defensive or offensive play where the whole team, or some unit within the team, acted together in concert to accomplish some goal. Perhaps they'd learn to move the puck out of their end zone and pass it up to a forward to take across the center line.

It was also the area where they had their least success. They drilled teamwork Tuesday. They drilled teamwork Thursday. By game day it was a shambles. From opening whistle to final blast of the game horn, two defense players and three forwards skated all over the ice—sometimes chasing the puck, sometimes trying to get out of the way, and sometimes just going over to wave hello to Gramma and Grampa sitting in the stands.

"Kevin, fall back. Set up the defense," Coach Milt Gorman would yell.

"Pass, Larry, pass," all the parents would yell, knowing Larry had never managed to skate more than ten strides without losing the puck.

The only parents not urging Larry to pass were his own. "Shoot, Larry shoot," they'd yell. It mattered not where he was on the ice. "Shoot, Larry, shoot" was their mantra. This, Alan discovered, was immediately cataloged by Larry's mother as a shot on goal. Count was kept, and while parents waited in the warm canteen for their sons to emerge from the locker room, postgame parental analysis was filled with lines such as "Did you see Larry tonight? Seven shots on goal. Seven!"

Alan was incensed. “The parents are worse than the kids. They ruin all the work we do at practice,” he protested to Milt.

“Even worse, they elect the league governors,” Milt said with a laugh.

“But look, Alan. These parents are pretty good parents, and the fact is that most of these kids are going to turn out all right no matter what we or their parents do. I only hope something of what we teach them will stick.”

One player who stuck like glue to two of the three teachings was Timothy Albert Burrows. Tim knew the rules and traditions. He also understood that he had a position to play, a particular job to do. When his teammates scrambled up the ice en masse, Tim, playing defense, held back, covering his area, ready to challenge an opposing breakaway or intercept a puck being dumped down the ice and pass it back up to a forward.

The trouble was, when it came to skills, Tim was terrible—the worst skater on the team and the least likely to get his stick on the puck if it did happen to slide nearby. As for successfully challenging a breakaway, forget it. Tim would make a valiant attempt, but by the time he arrived, the aggressor was long gone. Should fate by some miracle put Tim directly in the way, it was no great feat for the opposition to skate around him.

It didn't matter to Tim. He viewed life as endless joy. He radiated happiness.

"Tank top, you had 'em. You had 'em," Tim would enthuse after the game. "Remember how you deeked out number seventeen behind the net? He never saw that puck!"

Tim had total recall of every move his teammates made and the gift of genuinely cheering each success. He also had the good sense to refrain from mentioning their far more numerous screwups, a maturity level not shared by his teammates who, when finished with bad ice, bad refs, and bad luck, invariably began to catalog each other's sins—especially those of Jerry the goalie. If the team lost 9 to 2, it stood to reason that they would have won if Jerry had shut out eight of those goals.

"No way," Tim would protest. "We just needed to score eight more times! Jerry, you were great in the net tonight." Few ten-year-olds were willing to speak up against their peer group's common wisdom. Tim might be a nice kid, but he was no pushover.

"Who is this Tim?" Alan asked Milt after his second game as a coach.

"Not sure," said Milt. "I only wish the rest thought like Tim, and Tim skated like the rest of them."

"His stick doesn't look so good. Could that be part of the problem?"

"Perhaps. I doubt his skates are sharp. Not much money at home, I'd guess. I do know he doesn't have a mom. I understand she died about three years ago. Billy tells me Tim's dad works in a fancy restaurant. He rarely makes it to a game. Nice guy, though. I guess that's where Tim gets it from."

Wherever Tim got "it" from, "it" was special. Opposing coaches, watching Tim play, could never understand why it was Tim who wore the big **C** on his uniform shirt, the sign of the team captain elected by his fellow players.

Down in the locker room Tim dawdled as he always did while others hurried to change. Tim wanted to be last. Then he wouldn't have to make up some excuse to turn down a ride or, worse, be pressured into accepting. It was night, and he wanted to walk alone. Ever since his mother died, night was Tim's special time.

Lying on the front parlor couch several days before her death, Tim's mom had done her best to prepare him.

"We're all made up of two parts, Tim—our soul and our body. My body is not working very well, and when it stops, my soul will have to find a new home."

"What's a soul?" Tim had wondered.

"That's who we really are. It starts with love. God's love makes my soul come alive. It's like when we light a match for the barbecue: *poof!*" said his mom, throwing her hands up and giving Tim the best smile she could.

"No matter what happens to my body, I'll always have your love and God's love, so I'll always have a soul."

“And Daddy’s and Grandma’s love, too,” Tim had said seriously.

“Yes, Grandma’s and Daddy’s, too,” she replied softly, struggling to keep her emotions in check, knowing a fearless show of calm acceptance was the last and greatest gift she could give Tim.

Her next words were the reason Tim now peered into the canteen to be sure everyone had gone before slipping out the door into the night, hockey stick over his shoulder and skates dangling down his back: “When my soul is with God, it won’t have a body to help me talk to you, but I’ll always be with you whenever you want me.”

Tim looked puzzled.

“Right now I can’t be anywhere except where my body is. When I’m with God, if you want to talk to me, you can talk to me anytime, and I’ll hear you. I won’t be able to talk to you, but I bet if I ever want to tell you something, there will be a way. And you know the best part, Timmy?”

“No,” said Tim. He was seven, old enough to think that there wasn’t anything good about this conversation, much less a best part.

"You'll never have to worry about the dark ever again," his mother said. Tim was a child who was frightened of being alone in the dark. "I'll always be with you at night. You can talk to me anytime, Tim, and I'll hear you—even if you haven't spoken. I promise I'll always be with you, especially at night. Okay?"

"Okay, Mom," Tim said.

Six days later his mom died, lying on the same couch, surrounded by Tim, his dad, and a nurse.

The night of her funeral Tim slipped out the back door of his house and away from the crowd of friends and neighbors. Summoning all his courage he stepped from the porch, out into the dark.

Silhouetted against a deep, black, country sky lit with thousands and thousands of sparkling stars, the gentle low hills of the northern prairies rolled off to the horizon in every direction. Bravely but cautiously, Tim moved out to the edge of the yard and stood in the tall prairie grass.

"Mom?" he whispered. "Mom?"

Nothing. Silence. Black.

Tim looked up and tried again, this time louder, and more urgent. "Mom? Are you here?"

Tim's answer flashed high in the sky above. A brilliant hot white blaze appeared in the constellation Leo and streaked across the heavens before burning out on the far side of Orion.

Some would say it was God's hand. Some, that it was simply several grams of intergalactic rock ending a billion-year saga of aimlessly circling through space. For a seven-year-old boy alone, frightened, and with a broken heart the answer was unequivocal. Mom had said hello. His mother was with him. In that instant his heart began to mend, his fear lifted, and the night became his friend.

Tim told no one—not of that night nor of his ongoing conversations with his mother. He rarely heard from her, but if it was important, she'd send a message. And when she didn't? Well, Tim decided, it apparently just wasn't important enough.

When his dad, who worked nights, suggested Tim fill three evenings a week with hockey, Tim wasn't at all sure he wanted to. That night when Tim went for a walk to talk to his mother, it began to snow, the first snow of the season. Returning home, the snow reflected every speck of light, giving the night a soft glow, and Tim knew his mom had sent a message: play hockey.

Tim's delaying tactic in the locker room allowed him to again leave alone, and as he walked home, he talked with his mom and brought her up to date. One reason Tim kept a positive perspective on life and saw the best in others was that he shared the worst news, as well as minor frustrations, with his mother.

Tim knew he didn't need to speak out loud to be heard, but sometimes, when excited, upset, angry, or puzzled, he found himself muttering to the night air. A stranger passing that night would have heard a young boy talking to himself. But he wasn't. Tim was telling his mother of his frustration with teammates who failed to play their positions. The logic of playing positions, passing the puck, and working as a team to score goals was evident to him. Tim couldn't understand why it wasn't clear to the others.

Tim's Riverbend Warriors may have been short on teamwork, but two nights later, Saturday, teamwork saved Tim's life.

CHAPTER 3

It took a minute before anyone realized Tim was hurt.

He had just scored his first goal. His teammates were dancing on their skates, arms and sticks thrust high in victory. Coaches whooped with joy. Everyone saw Tim go down. Kids go down all the time. They often lie there, perhaps wondering how it happened or contemplating the view from ice level. Eventually they get up. Tim didn't get up.

The right forward on Tim's side had, as usual, deserted his position and followed the herd chasing the puck down the far side. Coach Gorman had motioned Tim to move up and cover the forward spot.

Seconds later the puck burst out of the dense pack of players and shot across and down the ice to Tim, slowing down just enough that he was able to get his stick on it.

Tim began to move the puck up. Behind him the herd gave chase. Tim was nearing the goal alone—no one to pass to.

Suddenly Tim realized it was a breakaway. He'd have to shoot. Stick back, down, *crack!* The puck flew forward.

It wasn't a perfect shot, but the goalie wasn't perfect, either. The puck headed toward the goal, something few grade-five shots actually did, and slid between the goalie's legs at the precise moment the mass of players reached Tim from behind.

Tim had slowed to make his shot. His pursuers, opposition and teammates alike, didn't stop or swerve.

The hit sent Tim facedown across the ice. His helmet hit the boards and stopped him. It wasn't that hard a hit. He should have got up again, but he didn't.

The realization that something was wrong washed over everyone, players, coaches, and parents.

The cheers died, and in a silence broken only by the swish of boots half-running, half-sliding across the ice, coaches from both benches rushed to where Tim lay, sprawled and still.

You ride with him," Milt told Alan as the paramedics loaded the unconscious Tim, strapped to a special frame, into the ambulance eighteen minutes later. "I'll go find his father. Nanton will look after the kids, make sure their parents are home and know what's happened. I don't want any boy home alone."

In the ambulance Tim was attached to several monitors.

One attendant spoke into an unseen microphone: "Transporting ten-year-old male, hockey injury, unconscious, head hit guard wall, sending vitals." The ambulance leapt forward, sirens screeching for attention.

"Is he okay?" Alan asked anxiously.

"Father?"

"No. Hockey coach."

"He's stable. I don't know more than that. We're sending all his vital signs to a doctor at the emergency room as. . . ."

"Unit eleven, confirm have vitals on screen," broke in a woman's voice from a speaker overhead. "Head immobilized?"

"Yes, doctor," the attendant responded. Alan noticed that he was checking what appeared to be sandbags on each side of Tim's head.

"Twenty milligrams of codeine. I'll monitor. Let me know when you turn in. Emergency Response Team is scrambling and will meet you."

"Twenty milligrams of codeine," said the attendant, confirming the doctor's order as he injected the drug into Tim's arm.

"That will keep him sedated so he won't suddenly come to. We don't want him thrashing around until the ERT assesses him," explained the attendant to Alan.

The ambulance suddenly halted under a heated canopy lit by bright yellow mercury vapor lights. The back doors were yanked open. Hands reached in, loosened the stretcher clamp, and Tim slid out.

By the time Alan scrambled down, Tim and his handlers were disappearing through swinging doors. Alan rushed after them as they wheeled Tim into a room and began transferring him from the stretcher to a hospital gurney.

Alan, unsure of what to do, entered as the door shut behind him. He stood silently against the wall. In the brightly lit room he wasn't hidden, but the swarm of green-garbed technicians, doctors, and nurses didn't pay any attention to him as they feverishly worked over Tim to assess his condition.

Alan recognized the doctor by her voice. On the ambulance radio there was a distinct Irish lilt to her words. The accent was all that gave her away, however. Everyone on the Emergency Response Team was dressed in the same shapeless green operating-room-style pants and shirts. Nets covered hair, masks hung around necks, and most jacket pockets had a clipped-on pager. When needed, they used names, not titles, and it was impossible to tell who, if anyone, might be in charge. Each seemed to know exactly what to do and instantly let others know what was happening. Decisions were made, but it seemed to be the group, rather than one individual, who made the decisions. Just what the process was Alan couldn't say. It was as if they worked in unison instinctively.

An X-ray machine swung out from the wall and hovered over Tim. The doctor and two others consulted a monitor and asked several times for the machine to be repositioned. From what Alan was able to understand, Tim, although still unconscious, didn't have a skull fracture or broken neck or back.

"All right, let's get him into MRI, stat!" As the group moved away from Tim, Alan was spotted and politely but firmly hustled out to the waiting room. Tim was rolled off through another door.

Twenty minutes later Tim's father arrived, accompanied by Milt Gorman. Just then the woman Alan had identified as the doctor came across the waiting room.

"Mr. Burrows?" she asked.

"Is he all right? I'm Burrows."

"Your son's had a bad accident, but we're very hopeful he'll recover completely. Right now, though, he's unconscious. He has a subdural hematoma pressing on his brain. We have to relieve the pressure. I've called in Dr. Nancy Cantor. She's an excellent neurosurgeon."

"Operate?" said Tim's father, his voice quavering as he tried to cope with the news.

"Dr. Cantor is very good. I'm sure Tim will do just fine. He's young and strong, but we have to relieve the pressure. You'll need to sign some papers."

"Yes, of course," said Tim's father, and he followed the doctor to the admitting office.

Alan and Milt sat down to wait. Two hours later they were still waiting, with Tim's father, for word from the operating room.

The smile on Dr. Cantor's face told the only story that mattered as she crossed the waiting room: Tim was alive and doing well.

"Your son's doing just fine," said Dr. Cantor. "They're moving him to intensive care. You'll be able to see him shortly."

The operation had gone smoothly. The problem was exactly as predicted. The only question now was when Tim would regain consciousness. The anesthetic would soon wear off, but he might not be conscious right away. It might take some time.

"Hours? Days?" his father asked.

"We don't really know," replied the surgeon.

Left unsaid, but as clear as if it had been, was the possibility that Tim might not regain consciousness. As if reading everyone's mind, Dr. Cantor said, "It may take Tim some time to recover. I'm not concerned. I don't think you should be."

"Thank you, doctor," said Tim's dad. "Thank you for saving Tim's life, I guess."

"My role is really quite small," the doctor said. "The people in emergency and in the ambulance do whatever saving needs to be done. Then the assessment team tells me exactly what to do and what to expect. I had a team of ten in the operating room with me, and every one of them played a vital role. Right now the team in intensive care is looking after Tim. I appreciate your thanks, but I want you to know I'm just one member of a team. We all depend on one another."

With that the doctor suggested Tim's dad visit his son. A bed in a family area next to intensive care was available for him to spend the night. Milt offered Alan a lift home.

"Did you hear that doctor?" Alan said, speaking to himself as much as to Milt as they got in the car. "She really was sold on teams. And she's a hot shot surgeon! Things sure have changed. I had a girlfriend once whose dad was a surgeon. He thought he was God. He didn't have team members in the OR. He had servants!"

"Things *have* changed," said Milt as he turned onto Alan's street.

"The surgeon we met tonight is an example of an effective team leader. Her goal isn't to be boss and make sure everyone knows she's in charge. It's to do whatever it takes to help the team perform well. If necessary, she can lead and take charge, but if others have better knowledge or skills, she is delighted to step back and let them take control. She'd rather see the team do well than be boss."

"You learned this selling bottled water?" asked Alan.

"When it's slow, you get lots of time to read," Milt said with a laugh. "I've always been fascinated by management books."

Alan sat quietly for a moment after Milt stopped the car in front of his house.

"Being the leader isn't the issue, is it?" said Alan thoughtfully. "What that surgeon was really talking about tonight was being a helpful team member. Everyone on her team, including herself, has to be focused on the success of the team rather than on his or her own success. Each of them works to serve the common good.

"There's no room for even one prima donna. Everyone's loyalty has to be to the team! That's their only reason for being."

"That's right," said Milt. "But beyond that, the group can't be successful just helping each other and working as a team. They have to serve their patient. They are held together by a compelling purpose—saving lives."

"Good point," said Alan.

"Unfortunately," said Milt, "people sometimes get so caught up in the process or working out the best leadership style that they forget what they're supposed to be doing in the first place. You see it a lot in hockey—not at the grade-five level, of course, but with some of the more senior teams. Beautiful plays. Lots of passing. Everyone playing position. But they don't score. As I said, organizations can get so focused on beautiful processes that they forget what they're really supposed to be doing. Getting it right starts to get in the way of getting it done."

Alan lay awake in bed that night thinking about Tim, the emergency room scene he'd witnessed, and the doctor's words. Tim really had been saved by a team. The doctor said it was the MRI scan that told them what had happened and showed what she had to do. "I may have done the surgery, but that MRI is the real hero and I don't have any idea how to run that machine," the doctor told Tim's father.

By the time Alan finally fell asleep, he had grasped what the doctor had told them: the medical staff, acting as a team, not individually, had saved Tim. They couldn't have if they'd acted as individuals. It was the total interdependence, the pooling of skills, that made the difference. Further, Alan believed the doctor was right about another point: no *one* skill was more important than another one. Ultimately, an individual skill reaches its potential when combined with other skills.

That was fine for medicine, but it was different in business, Alan told himself. But for the first time in his life he wasn't so sure. A chink had opened. He clung to the idea that business was different, but then at one time he had believed that flying in the air force was different, too. However, if he accepted the doctor's logic and applied it to his air force experience, his success as a pilot wasn't only because of his skill in the cockpit or even checking weather forecasts.

In the end it was because he was part of a team: the mechanics who maintained the engines, the people who had designed the plane, the workers who had riveted the fuselage, the ground control, his navigator—the list went on and on. These were people he depended on, people whose skills were critical to making his individual skill of any use at all. He had known that these people were important, but he had always seen them as support people and never as members of a team whose contribution and importance were equal to his. Now Alan began to realize that he had been wrong about his pilot experience, and if he'd been wrong about that, was there a chance he was also wrong about business?

Alan had a troubled sleep that night. His wife assumed his tossing and turning was the result of the trauma of rushing Tim to the hospital and the subsequent surgery. It was, but not for the reason she imagined.

CHAPTER 4

Tim woke up on Sunday afternoon, and the doctors, who late Saturday night and Sunday morning spoke with calm assurance, now looked so relieved that Alan suspected Tim had been in more danger than they were prepared to admit, perhaps even to themselves.

The Riverbend Warriors were ecstatic when they heard the news at Tuesday's practice. While they were watching Tim's inert body being carried off the ice, the team hadn't seen injury = concern. They'd seen severe injury = dead. Now what was considered by adults a narrow escape was, for the boys, a joyous resurrection.

"Look at all that energy," Milt said to Alan as they watched Gus Nanton supervise skating practice. "Lord only knows what a loss we'll have Saturday when those supercharged, rugged individualists all go tearing off in different directions. Another beating probably," he concluded morosely.

"I'm not so sure," replied Alan. "Perhaps we can give them a focus for that energy and beat someone ourselves." His thought slipped into silence as he watched the boys jubilantly skate with Coach Nanton.

Skating practice over, the boys rested while Milt reviewed rules and traditions. Then Alan took up the subject of teamwork.

"Last week Tim was hit. That happens. The good news is that Tim will be out of the hospital soon. The bad news is that he probably won't be allowed to play hockey again this year."

Talk about raining on a parade! The boys had expected Tim to be back soon.

"I think we owe Tim," Alan said slowly, and then let it hang.

Whether it was reading all the teamwork books, his own experience, or intuition, Alan recognized that Tim's fall had also cracked the orderly world of each boy. Something had happened that shouldn't have happened, and all the Warriors were part of it. They needed to do something—something for Tim, something to make amends for what had taken place.

"Any ideas?" Alan asked.

Silence.

Again Alan paused quietly for a minute. The boys shuffled their feet and looked anywhere except at one another or the coaches. They didn't have an answer.

"I suggest we win the division cup for Tim," said Alan softly.

The division cup! No Riverbend team had ever won the cup. None had even come close. The cup was awarded based on the last ten games of the season, followed by a playoff by the top four teams. Early season losses wouldn't count against them. They had a chance if only they could get their act together!

It was, Milt Gorman later reported to his wife, "a cosmic goose of epic proportions." Feet froze, heads shot up. The division cup would be the perfect offering. The boys had watched countless hours of television and had seen enough Hollywood movies to know that this was exactly what teams did when a hero was wounded. Soldiers took the hill for their dying sergeant. Cowboys braved the blizzard to rescue the pet dog of the farm boy with the broken leg. And when a police officer was murdered, the FBI and state and city police banded together to solve the crime. They would be soldier, cowboy, policeman, hero. They would win the cup!

Energy was restored and hit a new high. The only doubters in the arena were Coaches Gorman and Nanton; knowing the team, they ranked winning the cup right up there with the likelihood of being captured by aliens. Alan didn't rank chances any higher, but he was caught up in the energy of the boys. They had no doubts. They would be victorious. At that instant, commitment was total and unwavering.

The only problem was that the Riverbend Warriors was still a group of supercharged, individual performers. The challenge would be to get them to understand that they could reach their goal only by working together. They would have to be willing to change their behavior. "Willing," though, wasn't a tough enough word. Giving up old ways for new ones was going to be difficult. It would require powerful motivation.

Alan took the team out onto the ice and began setting up and drilling two simple plays he'd discovered in a library book. His mind, however, was focused on how he could get the boys' commitment level high enough to make retreat from their goal difficult if not impossible. He didn't think that when the going got tough, these toughs would get going. He figured they'd be gone—on to the next thing and blaming bad refs, bad ice, and bad coaching for their failure to win the cup.

"Too bad they aren't a little older," thought Alan. "If they were, I could get them to do it for their girlfriends." Showing off for the girls had certainly motivated Alan!

Then it hit him. It wasn't the showing off that was the real motivator. It was bragging about how good you were—in a low-key, cool sort of way, of course—and then having to deliver the goods or face the agony of failure in public. It was the commitment to others, a covenant, that really motivated. These boys might not have girlfriends, but they had parents, coaches, teachers, one another, friends, and classmates. A covenant with all these people to perform would make it difficult to back out, on the one hand, and would be a great motivator, on the other.

Like bicycle riding, skating was something that, once learned, stuck. As Alan skated he found that his blades slicing against the ice sang a long-forgotten rhythm.

Kish Boom, Kish Boom,
Kish Boom Baa.
Central High, Central High,
Rah! Rah! Rah!

His old high school football cheer.

That was it! They needed a cheer!

Not one for cheerleaders but one for the boys to chant to covenant with one another and whoever else was listening.

"Can you take them for a couple of minutes, Gus?" Alan asked as he skated to the bench.

While Gus went out with the team, Alan picked up the coach's clipboard and turned to a clean sheet of paper. Five minutes later he had it. The cheer:

Pum Nim, Kat Nim,
This Is Our Pledge To Tim.
Keemo, Kimo, Derrah, Stamps,
Riverbend Will Be The Champs.

"Pum nim? Kat nim?" Milt laughed

"You write a cheer," Alan said. "The point is, if the boys chant this at every practice and every game, at home and at school, they're on the line."

"They are that," agreed Milt.

The boys loved it. It had a primal rhythm. They bellowed out, "Pum nim, kat nim," as if it made sense. "Keemo, kimo, derrah, stamps" was chanted with hockey sticks drumming the ice in unison.

From now on, the coaches decided, the Riverbend Elementary School grade-five boys hockey team would begin and end every practice and game with this cheer. And with every repetition the boys renewed their covenant with parents, coaches, schoolmates, and one another.

That night after he told Susan about the new cheer and their goal of winning the division cup, Alan said, "I've got to get looking for a job."

"Wrong move," said Susan earnestly. "You have a huge severance package and lots of time to find a new job. I haven't seen you so happy in years, Alan. I think you need time to recharge your energy, and hockey coaching is doing it. There are lots of jobs but just one division cup. I say go for it."

Not working, not moving quickly to take control of a situation and again be master of his own destiny, was heresy to Alan. But after only a brief hesitation he agreed. Until Susan mentioned it, he hadn't realized how happy and excited he was. It had been a long time since he was this pumped up!

By game time Saturday, Tim was out of the hospital. Energy was high as they stood at center ice calling out, "Pum nim, kat nim, this is our pledge to Tim," before the game. After being crushed in a 10-to-3 defeat by the clearly better organized West End Raiders, the best the boys could muster was a half-hearted recital of the cheer as they dejectedly made their way to the dressing room.

The boys may have made a record fast transition from enthusiasm to disillusionment, but Tim's absence, and the corner they'd painted themselves into for all to see with the cheer, bounced them back to a grim determination to succeed. By the time the team left the dressing room, the coaches had restored some positive energy by pointing out that no team had ever won the division cup with a perfect record. Before they headed upstairs to waiting parents, the walls reverberated with:

Pum Nim, Kat Nim
This Is Our Pledge To Tim.
Keemo, Kimo, Derrah, Stamps,
Riverbend Will Be The Champs.

Driving home that night Alan considered the differences between his team experiences with the Riverbend Warriors and at work. The Warriors had Tim. Winning for Tim offered inspiration. Winning the cup was a quest for the legendary Holy Grail. A reason to be successful. The cup, like the Holy Grail relic for crusading knights, would by its very possession bring salvation to those who had it. At work, Alan's team had been just a collection of people with no overarching common cause—at least not one that anybody on his team cared about, and certainly nothing to match the quest for the Holy Grail.

In addition to their quest for the Holy Grail, the Warriors also had a covenant with one another, and with everyone else who had heard their cheer, to succeed. At work, Alan's team had had a few common goals, but they weren't their own goals. They were ones set by management. They might have been important to management, but they weren't of do-or-die importance to Alan. He also doubted that anyone else on his team cared that much, either. With the Riverhead Warriors, Alan may have proposed the division cup goal, but the boys had seized it as their own.

As Alan parked in his garage, he paused before getting out of the car. There was something else about the Riverbend Warriors and teams and himself, but he couldn't put his finger on it. This vague sense of unease, of a puzzle needing a solution, stayed with him until the next evening when Milt Gorman called to suggest a plan for Thursday's practice.

"Gus Nanton liked it. What do you think?" Milt asked Alan after outlining his plan.

"I like it, too," Alan said.

"That's great," replied Milt. "If these boys are going to have a shot at the cup, we have our work cut out for us."

Alan hung up the phone and stood a moment wondering about the call. Milt had never phoned before or even had a practice plan that Alan was aware of. His unease of the previous evening returned—the vague sense that he was missing something.

While he was turning off the house lights before going to bed, the answer came to him. It was so obvious that when he discovered it, he actually said, "Aha!" out loud, and his face burst into a smile.

Alan was again part of a team. Two teams, actually: the whole Riverbend Warrior team and, more particularly, the coaching team. Milt, Gus, and Alan were a team. They, too, had a Holy Grail: to teach these boys values, fair play, discipline, and teamwork—all skills they would need to survive and lead rewarding, exciting lives as contributors to their families, their community, and their country. Further, like the boys, the coaches had a covenant. They had written the chant and given it to the boys, thus placing the winning of the cup in the realm of the possible. Every time the boys chanted the cheer, the coaches' covenant with the boys, the parents, and one another—to prepare the boys to be winners—was further etched in the hearts and minds of all who heard it.

Like it or not, Alan was a team member again, only this time he didn't have the skills or knowledge to forge ahead on his own without Milt and Gus. Worse than that, they needed *him.* He had set this whole thing in motion, and without him, he was sure it would die. Milt, Gus, and the boys would revert to their former comfortable roles. There was no acceptable or honorable way out: Alan was a team member.

Alan spent another restless Tuesday night. He felt he was in over his head. For the first time in his life he had let himself get into a situation where going it alone wasn't going to produce results no matter how hard he worked. In fact, Alan didn't have any idea of what to do next.

On Wednesday morning he shared his troubles with Susan.

"I wish I could help you, Alan, but I know even less than you do about team building and how teams work," she said. "Too bad Miss Weatherby isn't still around. Weatherby's teams won more high school girls basketball championships than anyone. She'd know what to do, but I think I heard she died five or ten years ago. She was quite a lady and one fantastic coach."

"She was," agreed Alan, remembering the tall, thin, steely-eyed English teacher who had had far more success coaching basketball teams than she had drilling Shakespeare into Alan. "Weatherby must have been near retirement when we graduated. I don't recall hearing that she died, but you may be right. She'd be at least eighty now."

CHAPTER 5

Eighty-five, actually.

Weatherby was eighty-five, and her hands were curled with arthritis, but when Alan saw her later that morning in the lounge of the Park Manor Home, he realized he had forgotten that she had a way of wearing clothes that made even the simplest dress look stylish. A call to the Teachers Association an hour earlier had revealed that she was still alive, and they'd given him her address.

But how alive was she, Alan wondered as he crossed the room. And even if she was alert and aware, what help could she really be? A grade-five boys hockey team was very different from grade-twelve girls basketball. And if she did remember her coaching career, would anything she had to say work today? After all, her last championship was at least twenty years ago.

The Park Manor Home had an excellent reputation, and Alan knew it was one of the most expensive in the area. Weatherby, he decided, must have either lots of money or a generous insurance plan. It might have been expensive, but as Alan crossed the room, he was aware of how institutional it felt. The whole atmosphere of the place made him feel as if he was on a futile quest for assistance. He wondered if she would even know where she was.

Her hearing was sharp enough, however. As Alan approached, his footsteps alerted her. She was sitting slightly hunched forward. Firmly planted on the floor between her feet was a cane, topped by two arthritic, bony hands that pressed down as if to keep the cane from floating off. Hearing Alan's footsteps she looked up and squinted slightly to focus on him. Recognition flooded her face with a warm smile—and nobody could smile like Miss Weatherby. She was a beautiful black woman whose radiant face was stunning. Age, if anything, had only added to her elegance.

"Aha!" she said. "If it isn't the Foster boy. Brought me your essay, have you?"

Alan went from instant joy—he'd been recognized, so her mind must be fine—to instant disappointment. Essay? Her mind had gone. She was obviously living in the past.

"Hamlet and King Lear: comparison of two tragic heros, if memory serves me right," said Miss Weatherby.

Alan had reached her chair and now stood in front of her feeling like a naughty boy who hadn't done his homework. His first reaction was that this feeling was ridiculous. His second was much different.

The blush of embarrassment began in his ears and rapidly flushed his face. His memory caught up with Miss Weatherby's: the last week of the last month of his last year. All set to graduate but for one essay. And no time left to write it.

"Alan, you may not be an English scholar, but you're a nice boy," Miss Weatherby had said to him. "I'm marking your work complete."

Alan had stammered his gratitude and told her how much he really loved her class. Miss Weatherby broke in to say, "I hadn't realized you liked English so much, Alan. No doubt you'll want to do the essay just for the joy of it someday and hand it in."

Deciding he'd best shut up while he was ahead, Alan had made a hasty retreat from the classroom and fled down the hall. That was the last time he had seen Miss Weatherby. She remembered, and he'd forgotten.

"That's quite a memory," Alan said as he sat down across from her.

"When you're older, sometimes memories are all you have. You guard them all as precious," Miss Weatherby said with a wave of her hand toward several elderly people staring vacantly out the window. "That's what happens when you lose them.

"We came in here when my Jack started to go. This way we can be together," Miss Weatherby said softly. "That's Jack on the end."

Looking surprised, Alan said, "I didn't even know you were married."

"No reason you should. At home I was Mrs. Jack Gow, but at school after I got married, I kept Miss Weatherby. Except that everybody, even the principal, called me Weatherby. No Miss. No Mrs. Just Weatherby. I liked that.

"But what are you doing here? I don't see you carrying any essay for me to mark. You look as though you were expecting to find me here, so I take it that you've come for a reason."

It took Alan twenty minutes to tell her why. His story was often interrupted by questions from Weatherby, but not once did she interrupt with a comment or offer any advice. When he was finished, the two sat together silently for a few minutes. Finally Weatherby spoke.

"A team is a wonderful thing, Alan. It allows us to achieve things far beyond our own ability, while at the same time it keeps us humble." Again she fell silent before speaking.

"You get old, you get religious. I read the Bible every day, Alan. The lady in the suite next to ours teases me and says I'm cramming for my finals. But even when I was young, right from the time I started coaching basketball, I've believed that teams are one way God sends us proof. I'm real. I exist."

Alan looked surprised and puzzled. He had come looking for a way to help some ten-year-old boys put a black rubber disk in the net, and somehow he'd wound up in the midst of what he worried might become a religious lecture.

"I don't think I'm a religious nut, Alan, if that's what you're wondering," said Weatherby, reading the expression on Alan's face. "I'm not going to try to convert you. You'll convert yourself if any converting is needed. All I want to do is be clear at the outset where I'm coming from. If we're going to work together, you need to understand that, for me, teams are more than just a collection of people. I happen to believe a divine spark is the difference between a crowd and a team."

Intrigued, Alan asked, "Can you explain?"

"I can talk about it, certainly. But explain? I don't know. But here's how I see it. At the very instant I lay down my ego and recognize a divine connection, I begin to place others first. When that happens, I'm suddenly transformed. I've gone from being a relatively powerless individual to being part of something far more powerful, productive, and successful than I could be on my own. It all hangs on ten short words. Only three of them have more than two letters."

Then Weatherby uttered the words that would alter Alan's life forever:

None of us is as smart as all of us.

Alan knew from the way she had said it that he'd been given a key, perhaps *the* key, to Weatherby's success.

"That's the essence of a team, Alan. The genuine understanding that none of us is as smart as all of us. Remember I said the team experience was humbling? Well, once you accept that none of us is as smart as all of us, you can begin to put your needs, your pride, your agenda on hold and let the team's needs, pride, and agenda become your priority."

"Well," said Alan. "Will you help us build that kind of team?"

"I'm an old lady cramming for her finals, Alan. I've been in this home long enough to know the signs. My Jack is on the downhill slide now. It won't be long till he goes," Weatherby said as she looked over with love and tenderness at her husband.

"When he's gone, I'll be ready to go too," she said in a quiet voice. Then she turned her head toward Alan and, with a sudden brilliant smile, added, "But, Alan Foster, before I go, I'm up for one more championship!"

With that her right hand shot up off her cane. Thin, knobby fingers uncurled and splayed out from her palm as she gave Alan the high-five sign.

"All right!" said Alan with a burst of enthusiasm as his right palm met hers.

Alan had told Weatherby of the chant, and she proved that her short-term memory was as excellent as her long-term one. With Alan joining in she chanted:

Pum Nim, Kat Nim
This Is Our Pledge To Tim.
Keemo, Kimo, Derrah, Stamps,
Riverbend Will Be The Champs.

Having finished, Weatherby said, "And may I suggest a new ending:

Wear Ah, Tare Ah, Tanie Gleem,
Warriors Are A High-Five Team.

"A high-five team! I like that," said Alan and he again raised his right hand and joined his palm to hers in a high-five salute.

"I like it, too," said Weatherby. "It was after you graduated that those two lines were added to the ending of our school cheer. Think about it. The instant our hands touch we receive energy from each other. You can't high-five all by yourself. It takes a team of at least two, and both have to do it to make it happen. And when it does, it's a magic moment. It's the same when a team clicks; it's magic. I've always thought *high five* symbolized *a great team functioning perfectly and producing magnificent results*."

“Sounds good to me,” said Alan. As if cued by a conductor, they spontaneously began to chant again—this time all the way to the new ending:

Pum Nim, Kat Nim
This Is Our Pledge To Tim.
Keemo, Kimo, Derrah, Stamps,
Riverbend Will Be The Champs.
Wear Ah, Tare Ah, Tanie Gleem,
Warriors Are A High-Five Team.

Across the room, and almost in unison, the people who had been staring zombielike out the window turned and looked at the two of them chanting the cheer. Alan noted that Jack was the only one who smiled.

CHAPTER 6

Late the next afternoon Weatherby strode purposefully out of the Park Manor Home the instant Alan pulled into the driveway. He was glad to see that after the recent light dusting of snow, she walked with her left hand firmly on the railing that the home had installed for its occupants. The cane in her right, however, wasn't on the ground. Instead, she held it up waist high, off to her side, tip resting on the garden fence. She playfully knocked the snow off the fence's top rail as she walked along.

Alan pulled the car to a halt and quickly whipped around to open her door.

"I'll drive," Weatherby announced in her best schoolteacher voice that left no room for argument.

"Drive often, do you?" said Alan hopefully.

"Haven't been behind a wheel in years," said Weatherby.

"License?" croaked Alan.

"With my eyes? You gotta be kidding. They lifted my license years ago."

Alan began to mumble something about insurance as Weatherby climbed into the passenger seat. "Got ya!" Weatherby said, laughing.

"Let's take a look at this hockey team of yours," she added, buckling herself into her seat while giving Alan, standing at her door, a smile of such delight that Alan couldn't help but grin back.

"It's been a long time since I had anything to do with teams," she said as Alan drove to the arena and Thursday night hockey practice. "You warned the other coaches I'm a bit rusty?"

"They're thrilled you're coming. We need help. You know more about teams than any of us."

"Well, I've sure seen lots of them. When I was teaching, I used to work every Saturday with Jack—first helping him build the business and then later, after it was successful, helping to run it. Central Castings, over on Jackson. You may have heard of it."

"Sorry."

"No? Never mind. Doesn't matter. Point is, I also worked there for three years after I retired, and I can tell you I saw sales teams, production teams, and teams about teams at that place. At school we had sports teams, teaching teams, and task force teams to tackle specific problems. I've seen 'em all, Alan, and good teams, successful teams, all share four things in common, no matter what kind of team they are.

"Wear ah, tare ah, tanie gleem—four things you need for a high-five team," Weatherby sang out, and then burst into laughter.

"What did they feed you for dinner tonight?" Alan asked. "Must be some magical elixir. You're sure fired up and raring to go."

Alan wanted to know what the four hallmarks of successful teams were, but he couldn't help commenting on Weatherby's enthusiasm. Her head was high, her stoop gone, her face animated, and even her arthritic hands seemed better. She'd gripped her cane and whacked the snow off the fence with an ease Alan wouldn't have believed possible the day before.

"You're the elixir, Alan. At least this hockey team of yours is. Do you have any idea what it's like living in a home like that? Of course you don't. It's mind numbing. Every day it's the same routine. The only thing that changes is that every month some die and new ones come in. Park Manor is God's waiting room, Alan. I don't mind waiting and I don't mind dying. But it's hell on earth living without purpose, without meaning. You begin to think you haven't anything to give. When you've spent your life giving to others, helping others, and somebody comes along and says he needs your help, that's the greatest gift of all."

"I got involved for the same reason," said Alan. "I'd been fired, as I told you, and Milt Gorman said he needed me. It wouldn't have mattered if it was hockey or installing new showers in the locker room."

"That's one of the four keys to a successful team," said Weatherby seriously.

"Locker room showers?" joked Alan.

"No. Nice, but not necessary. Listen up. Here it is. *A sense of purpose—plus shared values and goals.* That's the first key to team success. If you don't have some good reason for being together that is important enough to get people fired up, as well as sharing values and goals, then you haven't a hope of ever having a great team. But you already know that. You know the difference between a team showing up to play hockey thinking it would be nice to win, and a team determined to win the division cup for an injured teammate. And it's even more powerful when a team has what I used to call a team charter."

"What's that?" asked Alan.

"A team charter is an agreement that clearly states what the team wants to accomplish, why its goals are important, and how the team will work together to achieve results. Actually, your cheer is a sort of team charter," said Weatherby.

"I've been thinking of it as a covenant. And the purpose—our reason for being—I've thought of that as finding the Holy Grail," said Alan.

"Good terms. But it doesn't matter what you call it. The essence is for people to have a strong enough purpose and share common values. Then they'll be willing to trade self for selflessness. It takes powerful motivation for people to put the good of the group ahead of their own self-interest. That's why you need a purpose—your Holy Grail—and a covenant or charter. The wonderful thing is that when you put the group first, all of a sudden your own needs get met better than when you were putting yourself first."

Weatherby fell silent, and Alan drove along thinking over what she'd said. He understood the importance of purpose, of a Holy Grail. The covenant process certainly seemed to be working for the Riverbend Warriors.

Weatherby's concept that "*None of us is as smart as all of us*" was a more difficult idea to accept. Of the ten people on his team at his last job, he figured he was smarter than the other nine put together. But even as he said this to himself, he could hear a second small voice saying, "And if you're so smart and they're so dumb, how come they're employed and you're not?"

It wasn't a comfortable thought. True, a couple of the others were smart enough, but three were as dumb as fence posts!

Alan was about to challenge Weatherby when he heard a strange sound, as if she were gasping for breath. Startled, Alan started braking. He was about to call her name when the rattling, rumbling, gasping sound hit him again, only louder. This time there was no mistaking it. A snore! A loud, deep, relaxed snore. Alan relieved his tension with a nervous laugh and eased the car back into traffic. He wasn't sure what to do, so he continued to the ice arena.

"We here?" asked Weatherby the moment Alan parked the car. Perhaps the crunch of tires on gravel had woken her.

"We are," said Alan, and then added, "You fell asleep."

"Always do in a car," said Weatherby with total unconcern as she opened her door. "That's another good reason not to let me drive. Now let's go see this hockey team."

CHAPTER 7

Their timing was perfect. Weatherby had no sooner been introduced to Milt and Gus than a loud clumping of skates on the ramp from the locker room to the ice, accompanied by a thundering rendition of the cheer, announced the boys' arrival. The ramp had concrete walls and ceiling. The floor was covered with a special hard black rubber sheeting designed to protect skate blades. The boys had discovered that the cheer echoed within these narrow confines and their young voices sounded like the roar of an army. It was their favorite spot to chant, and they gave it all they had as they rumbled up the ramp and burst onto the ice like a sudden thunderstorm.

The boys began the practice session as they always did, skating around the ice, first clockwise and then the other way, to limber up. At the whistle they headed for the bench.

If Milt and Gus were pleased but cautious welcoming the new coach, the boys were flabbergasted. Weatherby was ancient! Worse, Weatherby was a woman. They weren't hostile, just dumbfounded!

After Coach Gorman divided them into two squads and sent them out to play for ten minutes, their opinion altered slightly with Weatherby's sendoff.

"Let's see you kick ass," she hollered out with the volume and intensity of a barnyard auctioneer.

"Some old broad," one team member observed loud enough for the others to hear and with enough genuine awe that a tone of conditional acceptance was set among the boys.

"We have trouble dividing the players up evenly," Coach Gorman told Weatherby as the boys lined up for the first face-off. "Jed Boothe is not only the best player we have, but he's the only one who can skate, stick handle, and shoot straight. Whichever side has Jed automatically wins."

"He must be number twenty-two," said Weatherby as she moved a couple of rows higher in the stands for a sharper view of the game. "It's easy to see how much better he skates."

Coach Gorman's prediction was correct. Jed's squad won 4-0. All four goals were scored by Jed.

"Well, what do you think?" Coach Gorman asked Weatherby as the boys headed to the lockers after practice.

"Wrong boy wound up in the hospital" was Weatherby's blunt assessment. "We're going to have to get Jed off the ice for a while if we're ever going to win games."

Gorman and Nanton reacted with shocked silence. Alan was stunned, but for a totally different reason. He had never made the connection between Jed and himself, but with Weatherby's words he suddenly understood that Jed was doing on the ice what he had done at the office. Weatherby had come in from the outside and recognized a major problem, as had George Burton, the president of his former company.

"But he's the best we have," protested Coach Gorman.

"He's good. We'd be sunk without him," said Coach Nanton.

"He's a puck hog, though," said Alan Foster, "and I'm willing to bet Weatherby is going to tell us that we can't win games in a team sport if one player totally outshines the others."

"Not quite, Alan," said Weatherby. "You can have a player who is much better than the others. You can have a star. What you can't have is a star whose main goal is to look good himself rather than make the team look good. You called it being a puck hog. In basketball we used to say they were glued to the ball. Once they got their hands on it, the only focus they had was putting the ball in the basket all by themselves."

"Jed scores most of the goals," Coach Gorman pointed out firmly. "Without him we'd be in big trouble."

"You're in big trouble now," Weatherby said gently. "How much worse can it get than to be at the bottom of the league six years in a row?"

The question silenced all further objections. Weatherby was right. It couldn't be any worse.

"We might be able to work with Jed and turn him into a team player," said Weatherby. "But as long as he's out there, the other boys will defer to him. They'll never demand that he stick to the play plan, knowing he's more likely to score on his own than they will if he passes to them. And even if he did try to include them, they'd screw up. Then he'd get frustrated and go right back to playing the way he's playing now."

Alan again recognized the parallels between himself and Jed. Weatherby was doing a good job of describing exactly how he had handled himself before George Burton put him out the door.

"Seems to me we have trouble either way," said Coach Nanton. "We're losers with Jed playing puck hog, and we're losers if he tries to be a play maker because he'll go back to being a puck hog. We're sunk."

Weatherby replied, "No, we're not. You're assuming that because the boys mess up now, they'll always mess up. Get Jed out, and these boys will have a chance to *really* work on their skills.

"Right now you can drill them on skills, but they know it isn't for real. Come game day, Jed will take over, and they'll never have a chance to try in a game what they learn in practice. They won't even do it when Jed isn't on the ice. They'll just be killing time until you put Jed back in."

Coach Gorman looked over at Gus Nanton, and they gave each other a weak smile. Not long before, they'd talked about exactly this point. When Jed was on the ice, they could count on him to at least move the puck down to the opponent's end from time to time. Naturally the boys tried to get the puck to Jed, and then they coasted. Gorman and Nanton had further noted that when Jed was off the ice, the boys also coasted. Unlike Weatherby, their solution hadn't been to get Jed off the ice. Rather, they'd wondered how they might get him more time on the ice!

"You don't have to be permanently rid of Jed. You just need to send him away long enough to give the other boys a chance. Then when he comes back, with luck they'll have gained some confidence, and he'll be able to fit into the new way of doing things," said Weatherby.

"So how do we do that?" asked Milt Gorman.

"I haven't a clue," said Weatherby almost gleefully. "I'm in consulting here. Not management. I used to get the school to put my basketball prima donnas into the school play or something, and then I'd show my support for the arts by giving them a four- to six-week leave of absence from the team so they could be discovered by Hollywood. No one was ever discovered, but I sure put some teams together while they were gone. What you'll do, though, I have no idea."

"All right," said Milt Gorman cautiously. "Let us think about that. Is there anything else?"

"Driving over here I told Alan that all great teams shared four characteristics. The first is a sense of purpose, with shared values and clear goals formalized through a covenant or team charter. You have your purpose: winning the cup for Tim. The chant does a great job of formalizing the commitment. Your sessions on hockey traditions and fair play are the values they're to live by. I think you're in pretty good shape. If you can sideline Jed for a while, we can set goals for each player. Purpose, values, and goals—that covers the first significant trait of successful teams."

Weatherby fell silent, and after a minute Gus Nanton prompted her: "So where do we go from here?"

"Skills," said Weatherby. "That's the second key characteristic, the development of *high skills*. You have to teach skills and you have to *unleash* them. No sense in having great skills if you don't encourage the players to really go for it. To play high-five hockey they'll have to use every skill they have, and then you coaches have to push for a maximum effort. Skilled players with timid, cautious coaches won't create a high-five team.

"Skills are the foundation, though. A team can't perform if it doesn't know what it's doing. You have to start with individual skills. People need the basics, but that isn't enough. Everyone has to be committed to constant improvement—getting better and better at the basics every month, every week, every day. That means you have to be able to measure and compare in some way. It was easy in basketball to measure successful foul shots, but other skills weren't so easy to measure. For those I'd make a judgment call and assign a rating. Sometimes I'd give a player a score, a number. Sometimes I'd just tell them how they were doing. The important thing is team leaders need to measure improvement and give feedback."

The coaches listened to Weatherby with respect. She spoke with a firmness and clarity that left no doubt she knew exactly what she was talking about.

"Then what do we do?" Milt Gorman asked.

"Let's get under way with skills," said Weatherby. "Don't look so worried. I've lasted eighty-five years so far. I promise I won't die before the end of the hockey season. I'll tell you what to do next when we get to next. No sense complicating things. First you have to send Jed into limbo. Then we'll work on skills.

"As for you," Weatherby said, thrusting her cane tip toward Alan. "It's time I was getting home. If I stay up too late, this Cinderella turns into a pumpkin."

Milt said to Alan, "You look after Weatherby. I'll take David and drop him at your house." Then turning to Weatherby, he said, "It's been great to meet you and have you here. I'm looking forward to next time."

As Alan drove Weatherby home, he wondered what they might do about Jed. The minute the car started to move, Weatherby fell asleep, so he had lots of time to think. Bumping Jed had him worried. He knew how he'd reacted to being bumped, and he wanted no part of doing anything similar to Jed.

Alan needn't have worried. While he was driving Weatherby home, Jed's dad was meeting with Milt and Gus outside the locker room.

"Grounded. No sports. No movies. No television," Mr. Boothe announced to the two startled coaches.

Seeing the shocked expressions, he added, "I'm sorry. I know Jed's important to the team, but his schoolwork comes first. I warned him that if his report card wasn't better this time, he'd be grounded and spend his time studying, not playing. If he improves after the midterm exams, he can come back to hockey. I hope you're not too upset."

Gus Nanton was the first to recover from the shock. "Of course we'll miss him. Jed's a great player."

"I hope he'll be back soon," Milt Gorman added.

"I'm sure he will be," said Mr. Boothe. "Jed's a good boy. He just has trouble focusing on his studies sometimes. I'm sure this will be a good wake-up call."

The boys were starting to come out of the locker room as Mr. Boothe was leaving to fetch his son, saying, "Thanks for being so understanding."

“No problem,” said Milt with a straight face. “Schoolwork has to be number one.”

Milt’s straight face broke into a broad grin the second Jed’s dad rounded the corner. “Wow,” whispered Gus, his own face beaming with delight. “Fantastic,” Milt whispered back, and two hands instinctively shot into the air and smacked with pleasure in a high-five salute. “All right,” they both called out enthusiastically but in very soft voices.

Jed’s dad paused at the locker room door. Around the corner he could hear the two coaches whispering, no doubt trying to comfort each other over the loss of their star player. One was so upset that Jed’s dad could hear him smack the wall in frustration. It couldn’t be helped, though, he said to himself as he opened the door. Jed’s schoolwork had to come first.

CHAPTER 8

"Okay, boys, listen up," Coach Gorman announced in a booming voice after the boys had finished skating around the ice to limber up. It was Saturday, game day, and Coach Nanton had somehow managed to get an hour of precious ice time on Saturday morning for a hastily called special practice. Fortunately, the entire team with the exception of Tim and Jed showed up. The boys skated over to Coach Gorman.

"Here's the deal. We've lost two good men, Tim and Jed."

A rattling of hockey sticks on the ice indicated the team's agreement.

"Here's what we're going to do, men," boomed out Coach Gorman. Milt knew that boys liked to be referred to as men, whereas his male friends generally said they were going out with "the boys."

"It's going to be tough. But no one said it was going to be easy. We're down two good men, but we're still going to win the division cup for Tim."

Win the division cup? Without Jed? The players looked at their coach as if he were crazy.

"No, it's not crazy," said Coach Gorman, reading the expressions on their faces. "We have a secret weapon. Weatherby! I didn't mention it the other day, but Weatherby has won more state championships than any other coach in the history of this state." The coach conveniently omitted the fact that these had all been in girls basketball, not boys hockey. No need to bother the team with the details.

With that introduction the gate beside the penalty box opened, and out came Weatherby. To keep from falling, Weatherby had brought a walker with her, and she shuffled along clinging to the square aluminum frame, picking it up and moving it with each step. Move frame, shuffle. Move frame, shuffle. Alan walked beside her but respected her pride and let her walk on her own. Slowly but steadily Weatherby moved into position beside Milt.

"Today we're going to do only one thing," she told the boys in a surprisingly strong voice. "Stopping. Coach Nanton, a demonstration please."

While the boys' attention had been focused on Weatherby crossing the ice, Gus Nanton had skated down to the far end of the rink.

"No problem," he called out to Weatherby.

Short, fast running steps started Gus Nanton moving toward Weatherby. Then long, smooth strides built up power and speed. The faster he moved, the faster he pumped his legs. By the time he neared Weatherby, he was going full out. Several of the boys began to cry out, sensing a crash was inevitable. Weatherby held her ground and didn't flinch. At the last possible second Gus Nanton turned his body sideways and let the sharp steel edges of his blades cut deeply into the frozen surface, throwing up a shower of ice shavings. The blades ground deeper as he slowed over a three-foot slide, and then with a slight ankle twist to set them even deeper, the blades caught and held. Gus came to a sudden halt two feet in front of Weatherby.

The boys watched in awe as Weatherby, seemingly oblivious to what they'd seen as an escape from certain disaster, smiled at Coach Nanton and brushed flakes of ice off her sleeve.

"That was very nice," Weatherby said calmly.

Turning to the boys she said, "Stopping is the first skill we have to master. Once you can stop, you can afford to go fast. You can afford to cut in and steal the puck. Stopping puts you in control. If you're going to win, you have to be in control of the puck, and that means being in control of yourself. We're going to spend the rest of this hour practicing stopping."

Turning toward Milt, Gus, and Alan she said, "Gentlemen, the team is yours."

Before the practice she had made the three promise her one thing: no negative feedback. They could make suggestions for improvement to the boys but only after praising progress.

"It's simple," she told them. "To stop you have to turn your body sideways, and let the skate bite the ice. We can agree that every boy on the team has the strength to turn and push his skate into the ice. Right?"

The three had agreed.

"Question: Why don't they do it? Answer: Because they're afraid they'll get it wrong and go head over heels onto the hard ice. Right? Of course right. Our challenge is giving them the confidence to do it, not thinking that they need to be taught to turn and dig in. Your job today is to give them confidence.

"Remember, *what looks like a skill problem is often something else.*"

And so Milt, Gus, and Alan had the boys skate and stop, skate and stop. The boys worked on their own, and the three coaches moved from boy to boy, watching, praising, building confidence, watching again, and praising progress.

For ten minutes nothing happened. Nothing happened in fifteen minutes, either. At the twenty-minute mark the popcorn began to pop. All over the rink the sound of blades crunching sideways into ice could be heard, along with cries of "Hey, coach, did you see that!"

By the end of the practice every single boy was stopping properly. Several were trying to go fast enough and stop sharp enough to send a spray of ice shavings into the air.

The game that night was notable for several reasons.

First, Tim showed up. In a wheelchair and with his head swathed in white bandages, he was rolled into the locker room before the game by Alan. One by one the boys became aware of the wheelchair coming through the door. The bubbling enthusiasm of the ten-year-olds subsided. As Tim stood and walked slowly to his usual spot on the locker room bench, cheers, clapping, banging sticks, loud shouting, and questions greeted him.

"All right, boys, give him some room," said Alan. The boys may have heard, but they still swarmed around Tim until the five-minute warning bell sounded and they were forced to don their equipment and head for the ice.

"Go get them, guys," Tim called out as the team left the locker room. He sat back down in his wheelchair.

A moment later Alan noticed Tim's fingers gripping hard on the side rails of his chair as the boys' cheer echoed back down the ramp:

Pum Nim, Kat Nim
This Is Our Pledge To Tim.
Keemo, Kimo, Derrah, Stamps,
Riverbend Will Be The Champs.
Wear Ah, Tare Ah, Tanie Gleem,
Warriors Are A High-Five Team.

It was the first time Tim had heard it.

"The boys felt really bad about bumping into you, and so . . ." Alan began to explain.

"That wasn't their fault. It just happened," Tim broke in.

"Nevertheless, they felt bad," said Alan, leaving aside the issue of blame. Had the coaches done their job and taught stopping properly, as a confidence issue rather than a skill issue, might the accident have been avoided?

"Everybody wanted to do something for you, so we decided to win the division cup in your honor."

Tim couldn't wait for the night and the chance to tell his mom. In the hospital he'd had no doubt that she was with him all the time. She had said that if he ever really needed her, she'd be with him. He hurt. He needed her. Now that he was back home, there were times he was lonely, especially at night when his dad was at work and he knew the team was practicing or playing. But he didn't hurt now, and he was no longer frightened. He didn't need his mother so desperately, and the night was again their special time together.

Tim's arrival at the game was the first notable event, and the second was equally momentous: the Riverbend Warriors tied the game!

It wasn't the top team in the league—and the other team was missing two of its best players plus its best goalie—but the Warriors didn't have Jed, either. And they tied!

Without Jed to fall back on or to set the agenda, the boys began to play differently. Paradoxically, it was their stopping ability that really got them going. Weatherby was right. When they could control themselves, they could control the puck—at least better than they'd ever been able to before. Speed, agility, and digging into a clashing of sticks to grab the puck, they discovered, were all easier when they felt in control.

The only one missing from the game was Weatherby. "You don't need me" was all she'd say to Alan when he tried to arrange a time to pick her up. But she was there for Tuesday and Thursday practice the following week, and again they drilled basic skills: stopping, puck handling, shooting on the net, and passing.

The game on Saturday night was their best yet. Tim was in the stands, on crutches now, and Weatherby again declined to attend. They lost, but what a loss! The final score was 7 to 5, and in the third period they scored two goals and held the Northside Raiders to one. They won the third period—against one of the best teams in the league!

Alan phoned Weatherby, as he'd promised to, right after the game to give her the results.

"Fantastic. Tuesday we'll work on *individual goals* for every player. Then Thursday we'll move on to the third thing all great teams have in common."

"And that is?" Alan prompted.

"What we'll do Thursday," answered Weatherby. "Consultants charge by the hour. No sense telling you everything all at once."

Sure enough, on Tuesday they started setting out practice goals and game goals with each player. Weatherby recorded these in a three-ring binder, one sheet for each player.

Milt worked on the one for Jerry, their first-string goalie.

"Well, Jerry, what are your goals for a game?" asked Milt.

"Stop 'em all," said Jerry.

"Great idea." Milt laughed. "Let's put that down in big letters across the top. A shutout is a perfect game. What's a good game?"

"Let in three goals?" Jerry ventured.

"If there were one hundred shots on net, I'd say that was pretty good. But what if there were only four shots?"

"Not so hot," Jerry said.

"So let's try to set some goals for you based on what might actually happen. That way you'll know you've played a great game even if sometimes the puck goes in your net."

And so it went. Every player met with one of the coaches. Together they worked out specific performance goals for both practices and games, and these were written down. Weatherby found herself working with Larry, the one the coaches, among themselves, called Shoot-Larry-Shoot. Weatherby knew that, like Jed, Larry wasn't inclined to pass the puck once he had his stick on it. Unlike Jed, he didn't have great skills.

"Larry, how often do you think you should pass in a game?"

Larry looked puzzled by the question.

"Half the time?" ventured Weatherby.

"That might be all right," said Larry dubiously. Then he added in a much brighter voice, "If you're not on a breakaway, that is."

"That happen often? Breakaways?"

"Lots," said Larry with a big smile.

Alan, who had been standing nearby and listening to this exchange, also smiled, glad that someone else was working on goals for Shoot-Larry-Shoot.

Weatherby, after working with Larry on the exact definition of "breakaway," eventually had Larry agree to an 80 percent pass rate, including breakaways.

"How'd you do that?" said Gus as he looked at the sheets after practice.

"Trickery," said Weatherby. "We're tricking the other teams. If Larry passes eighty percent of the time and shoots twenty, they'll have a tough time anticipating what he's going to do. Smart man, our Larry. Most of the time he'll pass but then shoot when they least expect it. I told him his shots *on* goal may go down, but his shots *in* goal would certainly go up."

Although he didn't know it at the time, that evening Alan began a process that would lead to a new career. All he thought he was doing was entering into his home computer a list of all the things he'd learned about teamwork, beginning with George Burton's farewell line: *You do great on your own, but the rest of your team isn't doing very well. I need people who can work together for our goals. Sure, you'd score less, but the team would score a whole lot more.*

At the time Alan couldn't bring himself to agree with Mr. Burton. Now, Tim, Jed, Jerry, Larry, and Weatherby had taught him to understand what teamwork really meant. Reluctantly, he could see that Mr. Burton had a point.

CHAPTER 9

Thursday when Alan picked up Weatherby for practice, he eagerly asked the question: What was the third of the four keys to a successful team?

"I told you the first time you came to Park Manor to see me."

"You did?"

"I did. I think it was the wisest thing I said that day—or since, for that matter."

"I know," said Alan, remembering the single line he had put in boldface when he'd reviewed his computer notes earlier that day:

None of us is as smart as all of us.

"That's it," said Weatherby. "I told you then and I tell you again now: that's the essence of a team. The collective power of a group outshines individual performance. If people are focused on looking good themselves they can ruin a team's effectiveness. But if everyone puts the team first and focuses on making the team look good, the synergy is magic, Alan. I've seen it on sports teams, teaching teams, work teams, and sales teams. It was even true for the four-horse team my father had on his farm. When everyone pulls together, the results are always far better than the sum of individual performances."

Alan paused a moment to think. The sequence made sense. *First, purpose to get people fired up. Then skills so they can contribute to achieving the purpose.* And now . . . ? Harmony, Alan decided. *Synergetic harmony.* That's what this third key was all about. He was about to make that observation to Weatherby when the sound of a gentle snore drifted from the passenger seat.

As always, when the car's wheels ground to a halt on the gravel parking lot, Weatherby was instantly awake, out the door, and hustling up the ice arena walk.

Alan managed to reach the door first and hold it open. "So how do we convince the boys that none of us is as smart as all of us?"

"It's all in the cards," Weatherby answered mysteriously. She reached into her purse and pulled out six packs of recipe cards. She handed them to Alan, saying, "Here, you hold the cards. No shuffling, though."

Alan looked at the cards as they walked through the canteen toward the rink. Each of the six sets was the same, ten white cardboard index cards. Weatherby had numbered them with a heavy black marker in big numerals from zero to nine. Alan wondered what they were for.

"Tell the boys to be sure they're decent. Today's practice begins in the locker room. You rush on ahead and warn them that I'm coming. It will take me a few minutes to get down there."

Coaches and boys alike looked up with interest when Weatherby arrived. "Important question. Who are the best at math here?" she asked as she entered the room. "Last report card. Line up by marks. Highest mark at the door. Lowest down by me at the far end of the room."

The boys began comparing math marks and were soon in line, as ordered. All fifteen members of the team were at practice, and Weatherby divided them into the top eight and the bottom seven. Then she had Alan give a pack of cards to each of the top three math students and a pack each to the bottom three.

"No fair," said Taylor, who was in the bottom group. "They get the three best, and we . . ." He broke off, unsure how to say three worst without saying three worst.

"Slow group. You're the slow group," taunted a voice from the top eight.

"And you have eight, and we only have seven," Taylor said, more confident of how to voice this complaint.

"No, we don't," said Weatherby. "We have eight too. I'm number eight. All right, you top math boys, move over to the left wall bench. We'll sit on the right bench."

The boys went to their places.

"Here's the game," said Weatherby. "Coach Gorman is going to call out a number between zero and twenty-seven. Each side has to hold up three cards. The cards all have numbers on them. Those numbers have to add up to whatever number Coach Gorman calls out. The first side to get it right wins. You can talk. You can get help from other boys on your team. You can change a number after it's up. The first team to have three numbers that add up to Coach Gorman's number wins. Coach, call out a number whenever you're ready."

"Eighteen," called out Coach Gorman. Numbers flashed up, boys called out, numbers went down, arguments broke out. Weatherby paid no attention. She walked over to one of her team's cardholders and said, "You're Graham, aren't you? I thought so. I was watching you practice drop passes Tuesday night. You're really very good. Look. Here's what I want you to do. If Coach Gorman calls out a number from zero to eighteen you hold up zero. If it's nineteen or more, hold up a nine. Okay? Just use those two cards. Up to eighteen, zero. Nineteen or more, hold up nine."

"Sure thing," said Graham.

"If Coach Gorman calls out eighteen, which card do you show?"

Graham held up a zero.

"Attaboy," said Weatherby.

While she'd been talking to Graham, the top math students got their act together and with a seven, a two, and a nine had cards totaling eighteen. Weatherby paid no attention as Coach Gorman declared them the winners. Instead she went over to Andy, who also held cards for Weatherby's team.

"Let's play again," she said to Coach Gorman, and then quietly to Andy, "If he calls out any number up to nine, hold up a zero. Ten or more, hold up a nine. Okay?"

Just then Coach Gorman called out, "Twenty-five."

Again panic, shouts, advice, blame, and confusion rang out on the top math team's bench. But on Weatherby's bench Graham held up a nine and Andy held up a nine. Weatherby sat down beside Tony, the third cardholder, and said to him calmly, "If the number has one digit, hold up that number. If it has two digits like twenty-five, add up those two numbers and hold up that number. What's two and five?"

"Seven," said Tony.

"Then hold up a seven."

Tony did, and while the top math team flashed numbers and shouted in total confusion, Coach Gorman announced Weatherby's team the winner. The top math team couldn't believe it. As they were trying to organize, Weatherby told Tony, "Watch out, though, for nineteen. When nineteen is the number, you have to add twice. What's one plus nine?

"Ten," said Tony.

"Right. Now add one plus zero. What do you get?"

"One."

"Good," said Weatherby. "Hold up the number one if he calls nineteen."

Coach Gorman called out nine. Both Graham and Andy held up zeros and Tony a nine to win before the top math team even got started.

"Fifteen," called out Coach Gorman.

Graham flashed a zero, Andy whipped up his nine, and a moment later Tony, having added one to five, held up a six. The top math team sat stunned.

Before the next go-around the top team decided that Weatherby's team was going in order, so they tried it. Not knowing what the plan was, they were soon working at cross-purposes, losing every round and blaming one another for their collective failure. They became even more upset when Weatherby started to rotate the boys holding cards for her team. She even let cardholders teach new ones the method. "But do it quietly," she warned. "Keep the plan a secret."

Finally, after fifteen rounds, Weatherby ended the game and announced the results. "Final score: the top math team one, and the team someone called the slow group, fourteen. Not bad for a slow group!"

The slow group boys glowed with pride as Weatherby explained to everyone the system they had used.

"Here are the lessons I want you to learn. One, if you have the basic skills and a game plan, then stick to it. That's better than no plan even if you're the most skilled people playing. Two, the three boys with the lowest skill level can beat the three top boys if the three low boys work together and the three top boys don't. Three, skill is important, but once you have the basic skills, working together is more important than having better skills. Four, if you work as a team, you can beat the best there is if the best doesn't work as a team."

Weatherby paused a moment, and then she reviewed the four lessons again, this time winding up with: "All four are really the same thing. Just different ways of looking at it. I can give you one short sentence of ten words that sums it all up: *None of us is as smart as all of us.* Who can tell me what that means? None of us is as smart as all of us."

Aaron put up his hand.

"Yes, Aaron?"

"It means that no matter how big my brain is, it will never be as big as all the other brains on the team put together. And I guess it means . . ."

"Go on."

"Well, I guess it means that if I want to have the biggest brain possible, what I have to do is pool my brain with all the others—like linking a bunch of small computers together to make a big one."

"Excellent, Aaron. And what do you think that means for our hockey team?"

Aaron thought for a moment, then said, "It means that even if the other players on all the other teams are individually better than any of us, if we play as a team better than they do, we can beat them."

"Aaron, you're the smartest tiger in the jungle. That's exactly what it means. No matter how good they are as players, we can use teamwork to beat them. We can do out on the ice what my team did with the cards. We can make a plan. We can work together to execute the plan. If the other side doesn't have a better plan and stick to it, we have a good chance of winning no matter how good the other players might be."

Alan didn't mean to interrupt Weatherby, but when she fell silent he just naturally said, "Tell me, what would have happened when Coach Gorman called out seven if Graham, instead of holding up a zero, said, 'Hey, this is easy. I know I can score myself for sure on this one,' and held up a seven?"

"He'd have got it right, but the team would have got it wrong," said Jerry, who had been one of the cardholders on the top math team.

"Right," said Alan. "Graham might have got the answer right—we could say that he scored—but the team wouldn't have scored. Once you have a plan, you have to work it as a team.

"In hockey if the plan says you're to pass and instead you shoot and score, the team gets your score. But what happens the next time? Probably you don't score, and the time after that and the time after that. Provided you have a good plan, the team will always score more often by sticking to the plan even if it means you yourself score less."

"Coach Foster is right," said Weatherby. "Later on, after we've perfected following the plan, we'll talk about times you can make changes to the plan. Part of the plan of any great team is knowing when it's okay to change it because of circumstances or opportunity. But that's later. Now I suggest we get out there on the ice and start making plans to score lots of team goals."

Weatherby's final words, "Let's get fired up, guys," were lost in the thundering chant of the boys heading up the ramp.

Out on the ice, after the warmup skate, Weatherby had one more surprise for the boys and the coaches.

"Here's what I suggest," she said to the gathered team. "When you score a goal because of teamwork, that's like being top man on those human pyramids you see at the circus. The man at the top stays up there because of the people under him. And who deserves the most credit? The guys on the bottom, of course. They hold up everything.

"From now on let's count goals differently. We'll use the new system at every game to choose the most valuable player. The player who scores a goal will get one personal point. The one who passes it to him, the person who gets the assist, will get two points. The player who passes it to the person with the assist will get three points."

The boys thought this was a great idea. Jed, who until now had scored most of the goals, wouldn't have thought it a good idea at all, but he wasn't there. In his absence both the boys and the coaches enthusiastically adopted the idea of a most valuable player award and Weatherby's unique way of awarding it.

The rest of the session was taken up practicing plays and playing proper positions. They were all drills the coaches had tried countless times in the past, but now with a new perspective on what team play really meant and with Jed grounded at home studying, the team worked at a whole new level of dedication and enthusiasm.

"Once the boys have the basic skills and can use some simple set plays in a game, plus be counted on to play their positions, I suggest you start to rotate the linemen and defense players around a bit," Weatherby said to the coaches after practice. "Flexibility is important to a successful team. People need to be cross-trained and have a good idea of what other jobs are all about.

"Moving people around not only builds skills, but it also provides variety and gives team members a comfort level with change. You need a team that's adaptable, and people don't develop coping skills if they drift along in the same rut doing the same things in the same way for the same reasons."

"What about the goalie? Should we move Jerry, too?" asked Milt.

"Not for games, I wouldn't," said Weatherby. "Jerry is in a specialized skill position, and it's not reasonable to expect others to match those skills. It doesn't make sense to rotate the flight attendants and the pilots on a plane, either. But it does make sense to cross-train both pilots and flight attendants on different types of aircraft. Remember that you're aiming for flexible skills and flexible minds. With the team it wouldn't hurt to put each of them in goal every now and then during practice. If nothing else they'll gain some respect for Jerry."

"Sounds like a good idea," said Gus. Milt and Alan agreed.

"One other thing," said Weatherby. "With Tim out for the season we don't have a captain. I suggest we rotate that role. Part of the flexibility of great teams is the ability and willingness to share leadership."

"That's a great idea," exclaimed Alan, who then told them about watching the medical team the night of Tim's accident. "Seeing them in action was really something. Everyone was willing to play a leadership role when needed. They were focused on whatever it took to make the team perform well. Their energy was focused on being a helpful team member, and that meant sharing leadership."

Before anyone could comment, the boys started to leave the locker room, and the coaches said good night to one another.

As Alan pulled out of the arena parking lot, Weatherby took a rolled-up scroll of papers from her handbag, flattened them out, and handed them to Alan.

"Here, you'll want these for the Saturday game," she said.

Alan stopped at the parking lot exit and flicked on the car's interior light to see what he'd been given. It was a sheaf of certificates. Across the top was printed *Riverbend Warriors Most Valuable Player.* Under that was a space for the winner's name and a place for Alan, Gus, and Milt to sign as coaches.

"This is great," said Alan. "But there's no place for you to sign."

"I'm in consulting, not management, remember? But if I was managing, I'd do my darndest to see the name of Shoot-Larry-Shoot on the first one."

"Where'd you get these?"

"Made 'em up on my computer. We old geezers know a modern trick or two."

"You sure do," said Alan, turning off the light and driving away. "Before you drift off to sleep, I want to say something."

"Me sleep?"

"Yes, you. Unless my car has learned to snore."

"Jack put you up to this, didn't he?" said Weatherby. "I've been trying to tell him for years that I don't snore. But say what you want to say quickly, just in case I do drift off."

"I was thinking on the way over that your first key, *providing a clear purpose with shared values and goals,* is all about getting people fired up—putting some meaning and direction into a team's existence.

"The second key, *unleashing and developing skills,* contributes to achieving the purpose. The third key, *none of us is as smart as all of us*, is really about harmony, synergistic harmony.

"You still awake?"

"Of course I am."

"Good. Anyway, I can now see that '*none of us is as smart as all of us,*' is really about turning individual skills into team skills. I never understood it before—the reason teams can work so well is that by combining individual skills you create a whole new skill set, team skills. Individuals acting on their own can never have team skills."

"That's right," said Weatherby. "Your first thought was right, too. It is harmony, but you also recognized there was synergy. The total becomes more than the sum of the parts.

"It's like the two headlights on your car. If you cover one, the other goes how far? Say five hundred feet. But put both lights on, each one going five hundred feet, and what happens? Somehow they make things brighter in the first five hundred feet and then go further, perhaps eight hundred feet. That last three hundred feet, between five hundred and eight hundred feet out, can only be lit if they come on together. They actually gain energy from each other. I don't know how or why that happens, but it does."

"I don't know how it happens, either," said Alan. "As you know, I got fired from my job because I wasn't a team player. I was like Jed Boothe. I guess my light went six hundred feet. Better than the others who were at five hundred feet but no help to them. I wouldn't turn on with anyone else, so none of us made it to eight hundred feet."

After a pause Alan said, "It's really interesting, the parallels between a grade-five hockey team and teams at work."

"A team is a team, Alan. Work teams may be better at some things than sports teams, and vice versa, but in the end a team is a team."

Alan replied, "Sports teams generally seem better than work teams, at least beyond the grade-five level, although in many ways our hockey team is already better than the team I was part of at my job."

"Sports teams have been at it longer, Alan, I guess they have that edge," said Weatherby. "They're generally much better at keeping score of performance and giving and receiving feedback.

"Come Saturday we'll have a most valuable player award for each game. That gives the boys immediate feedback. Coaches don't wait for an annual sit-down with each player to go over goals and how they've done. Feedback is instant. Accountability is immediate."

"I guess coaches are tougher than bosses, but it didn't take our company president long to clear me from the bench."

"Toughness is only part of it, Alan. In sports, coaches are far more willing to invest in training and practice. You obviously had some great skills, and you're bright. All you needed was the right wake-up call. A coach would never waste talent like yours."

"Nice of you to say," said Alan.

"It's true. Sports people are excited about training. When I was working with Jack in the business, I found many of our competitors were reluctant to train. They worried that their employees would get good, and then one of two things would happen. Either they'd have to pay more money, or the employee would leave. What they didn't understand was that good employees were more productive, and so the company could afford to pay more."

"Seems obvious to me," said Alan.

"It is, and they knew it but didn't believe it. There's a difference between knowing and believing.

"The big problem, though, wasn't the money. What really scared them was that people would leave, and they'd have wasted all the money invested in training them."

"Sounds reasonable."

"It is until you understand the synergistic harmony we talked about earlier. Individual skills translate into team skills. Trained people take the team to new levels. That level becomes the norm. If a skilled player leaves, it can hurt the team, but the team will continue to function at a higher level than when it started. As the song says, 'You can't take that away from me.'"

"We're here," said Alan as he drove into the Park Manor Home. "You stayed awake the whole way."

"Only thing I like better than a snooze is talking," said Weatherby.

"So even if a knowledgeable person leaves, the organization or company keeps benefiting from his or her knowledge because it's been shared," said Alan.

"Shared, and the organization or team has learned to function at a higher level. That experience, that capacity, isn't lost when a key player leaves. It may be diminished, but it isn't lost."

Alan cracked his door open, which turned on the car's interior light. Looking across at Weatherby he said suspiciously, "And you've learned all this from teaching high school basketball and helping Jack run Central Castings?"

"Oh, that and a couple of other experiences," Weatherby said, opening her door.

"Come to the game Saturday?" asked Alan as he walked her to the door.

"Can't. But call me afterward with the score and pick me up for Tuesday practice."

That night when Alan sat down at his computer to update his list of lessons learned, he found himself wondering what Weatherby had meant by "a couple of other experiences."

Curious, he turned to the Internet in search of Lillian Weatherby. He discovered several old news stories concerning basketball championships and one written when she retired—nothing that would explain her remark.

He was about to exit from the Internet when he had an idea. He keyed in Lillian Gow and started to search. This time he hit the jackpot. Lillian Gow was listed as a past board member of the state power authority, a West Coast department store chain, a local bank, and a national airline. She had also served on the board of a steel industry association and a large parts manufacturer for the automobile industry.

At first Alan thought it must be another Lillian Gow. It wasn't, though. She had retired from her last board, the bank, five years before, at eighty.

A news story quoting the chairman of the bank, John Christie, told the story:

> I discovered Lillian Gow in school. She taught me English. I wanted a woman on the board and did a big business with teachers, so I thought a teacher would be a good idea.
>
> When Lillian agreed to join, she proved herself at every meeting to be the best prepared board member I had. She was also very shrewd.
>
> One of our other board members was on the state power authority, and he got her on that board. Next it was the department store chain, and it went from there.
>
> She might be famous now, but we had her first.

Alan's first thought was to tell Weatherby what he'd discovered. His second was that he wouldn't mention it at all. If she wanted to tell him, she would. If she didn't want to, he'd respect that.

CHAPTER 10

Riverbend Warriors, 6; Eastland Wolverines, 4.

That told part of the story.

The story behind the story was that just prior to the game Milt learned that Tim wouldn't be coming. He had been rushed back to the hospital with a severe headache. "He bled some from his nose," his worried father told Milt. "If it's a nosebleed, which he gets from time to time, that's fine. But with his accident and the headache, they want to be sure."

The boys would notice Tim missing, so Milt told them what had happened. Milt thought he'd have to give them a pep talk to perk them up, but Shoot-Larry-Shoot took care of that for him.

"Sounds like a good night to win for Tim," Larry said to the hushed locker room. "He won't have a headache when he hears we won."

There was a primeval rhythm and resonance to the chanted cheer that night as they burst up the ramp ready, willing, and more able than ever to do battle.

The team's most valuable player award was another part of the story that night. The coaches didn't have to fudge the figures. Shoot-Larry-Shoot was the clear winner. All game long Larry passed every time he had the puck. Except once. Early in the third period, with his parents frantic because their superstar son hadn't made one shot on goal, Larry found himself just to the side of Eastland's goalie when Roberto passed him the puck. Larry had a clear shot and scored. His parents went wild with joy.

Seeing his chance and knowing that parental pressure could cause problems with Larry's new style, Milt left the bench and walked over to where Larry's parents were.

"Great goal," he said. "Did you notice that Larry's playing a new strategy designed to help him score more goals? The idea is for him to pass unless he has a sure thing. That way we fool the other team. They expect him to pass, so when he shoots, they're caught off guard. His goals-scored-to-shots-taken ratio will go soaring. I wouldn't be surprised if he scores two or three times as many goals now."

Two or three times as many goals! The parents' eyes glazed over at the prospect.

Later that period Milt Gorman heard two familiar voices yelling out, "Pass, Larry, pass."

The big score of the game, however, came after the last whistle had been blown.

"Coach, you're doing a fantastic job," José Monterro's father said to Milt Gorman as the boys headed to the locker room. "All of a sudden they're playing like a team."

"Alan Foster's responsible for all that," Milt started to explain, but before he could mention Weatherby, Mr. Monterro turned, clasped Alan firmly by his elbow, and led him away, saying, "Mr. Foster, I'd like a word with you."

"Certainly," said Alan quickly trying to recall all the conversations he had had with José and what might be the problem.

"Teamwork," Mr. Monterro was saying. "We need better teams, and I think you're just the man to do it. How much would you charge for helping us?"

"Excuse me? Help how?" asked Alan.

"Teamwork, of course. My company needs you, Mr. Foster. I'll pay whatever's fair. You come out for an hour or two and tell us what to do."

"I'm sorry, Mr. Monterro. I've never done that," said Alan.

"Well, you do now. Name your price."

"I don't know. Really. . . ."

"How about . . ." Mr. Monterro leaned over and quietly whispered a figure to Alan that was about what he had been paid weekly at his last job.

"For a couple of hours?" Alan whispered back.

"Some morning."

"That's way too much," said Alan.

"I won't take no for an answer."

"I can't," said Alan.

"Of course you can. Look, here's the deal. You come and help us, and if I don't think you're worth every penny of it, I won't pay you. Now will you come?"

"I'll have to think about it."

"Fine. Here's my card. Call me Monday. And say yes. My company needs some of the team magic you've created here."

"But I've had lots of help. It isn't just me," said Alan.

"Of course it isn't," said Mr. Monterro. "I wouldn't expect a team expert like you to do it all on your own."

When Alan phoned Weatherby with the score, he told her about Mr. Monterro's offer. "Crazy, isn't it?"

"Not at all, Alan."

"But even if I could do it, with all you've taught me, the money is way too much."

"First of all, it's not what I've taught you. It's what you've learned that counts—from me, the boys, the other coaches, and the books you've been reading. Most of your learning has come from your own experience both at work and with the team. Experience is the best teacher of all.

"You've become a knowledgeable person, and that knowledge has helped take the team to a whole different level. It's just as we talked about Thursday night. Even if you left, the team isn't going to slide all the way back. That's why winning organizations and winning teams are continually learning. All you need to do now is go out and share what you've learned with others. You'll be a fabulous teacher, Alan."

"But it's too much money."

"Fiddlesticks! If you help Monterro create teamwork, I bet those new teams can make back your fee in extra profits in seven days. A one-week payback is a good financial investment."

"I don't even have the fourth key!" he protested.

"You do. You just don't know it," she teased. "Come Tuesday you'll know it."

On Sunday, Alan drove over to see Weatherby and brought along a printout of his computer notes. He dreaded the thought of making a two-hour presentation on teamwork. On the other hand, working with the team, teaching, and helping others be successful was the most fun he could remember. If he could do it for a living, that would be the best job in the world.

Weatherby reviewed his notes and gave him the same advice that Susan had. "You have lots of good material here, Alan. Best of all, you really understand what it means. I've watched you with the boys. You're a natural teacher.

"And one more thing. Believe it or not, you're a hero, an inspiration. People want to be part of a great team; they want to build great teams. You're living proof that it can be done—and no offense intended, but if a guy like you, who has been fired for not being a team player, can pull it off, that's proof they can, too. I say go for it."

So Alan went for it.

On Tuesday, Alan would learn the fourth key. On Wednesday morning at ten all 372 employees at Monterro Enterprises would be gathered to hear him speak on teamwork. Alan had tried to delay his talk a couple of weeks, but Mr. Monterro was adamant. He wanted Alan now.

CHAPTER 11

Tuesday was also the day Tim came out of the hospital. He sent word that he'd be at the game on Saturday.

"He said to give special congratulations to Larry on his award," Milt told the team in the locker room before practice. Hockey gloves went flying through the air, all aimed at Larry. Cheers, hoots, and calls filled the room—a strange but traditional way of indicating approval.

While the boys skated their warmup, the coaches gathered at the home team's bench.

"Well, Weatherby, it's time to tell us the fourth key to creating a great team," Milt said.

"None too soon if we're to win the cup, and Alan's going to do his presentation tomorrow," said Gus.

"Amen," said Alan.

"It's the three r's," said Weatherby. "What else would you expect from an old schoolteacher. Here it is: *repeated reward and recognition.*"

"Repeated reward and recognition," echoed Milt.

Weatherby said, "This key reinforces the first three keys. Every chance you get—and if you don't get one, you create one—you look for behavior that is aligned with the first three keys: first, purpose, values and goals; second, skill development; and third, team power, or 'None of us is as smart as all of us.'

"People repeat performance that garners reward and recognition. Your job is to keep the accent on the positive."

"Catching people doing things right," said Milt in a thoughtful way.

"Great concept. The only trouble is, it's tough to do on a daily basis," replied Weatherby. "First, we're not conditioned to look for things going right. Management and coaching are too often about catching people doing things wrong. The emphasis is on seeking exceptions, deviations from the way things are supposed to be, and correcting them. There is nothing wrong with catching a problem before it becomes a big problem, but organizations and teams would be better off if people worked to increase the number of things going right rather than always fighting the things going wrong."

"On the theory that if the boys do twice as many things right, they won't have time to do things wrong?" asked Milt.

"Something like that," said Weatherby. "Only it's more that if they do twice as many things right, then the occasional thing they do wrong isn't so significant."

"To get more things done right don't you have to stop doing things wrong? Sort of opposite sides of the same coin?" asked Gus.

"If all you have is a limited number of coins, then that's so," said Weatherby. "But usually you have lots of coins, lots of opportunity to create more of the good stuff, in addition to converting bad stuff to good."

"Instead of focusing on shots on goal that don't score, we should focus on those shots that do score," said Alan.

"Exactly. That and shooting more often. Focus on the positive. And the way you do that is by making sure the first three keys are always present, and that means repeated reward and recognition.

"There's another thing," Weatherby continued, "another reason. When you focus on the positive, you develop the habit of doing things right. I had a student once who later went to work putting up steel girders twenty or thirty stories in the air. I asked him how he could walk out on those beams. He said the trick was to concentrate on where you *should* put your foot and never, never, never think about where it was *wrong* to step. That guaranteed you'd do it wrong. By concentrating on doing things right, you actually wind up doing fewer things wrong."

Alan said, "We started to talk about looking for what you called alignment between what people did and a team's purpose, values and goals, skill development and team power. Is there a difference between alignment and doing something right?"

"Not really. But alignment is perhaps a lower hurdle. That's why I like to use that word. Doing something right is sometimes thought of as only being a significant positive move. Scoring a goal, for example. Staying in position and covering your area, even if the puck doesn't come your way, is also doing something right, but because it's not where the action is, people forget to recognize its importance to the team. And remember, recognition itself is often the reward."

"If we recognized and rewarded every player every time he was aligned . . ." Milt started to say, but Weatherby broke in to finish the sentence: "We'd be well on the way to winning the division cup."

"It's that important?" said Alan, half as a question, half as a statement.

"It's more than important. As I said, it provides support for the first three keys. You confirm your aspirations as worthy, you pay homage to the skills and knowledge of both the individual and the team, and you create a spark of energy that encourages people to focus on team success, not individual performance."

There was a short silence. On the ice the boys were finishing their warmup and began skating to the bench.

Alan said, "One last thing, Weatherby. By directing our praise to team aspirations, skill development, and team power, we will ensure a total focus on the team's mission. That, in turn, should cut down a lot of effort directed at wrong things."

"Absolutely," said Weatherby. "It happens all the time. People and teams get praised or pat themselves on the back for doing something that isn't aligned with where they want to go and how they truly want to behave. Then they get going in the wrong direction. Shoot-Larry-Shoot used to be a good example of that."

Milt said, "You're right, and what we did, when you think about it, was clarify the goal for Larry and his parents, and then use reward and recognition to redirect his behavior so that it was aligned with his new goal."

"Wonderful how it works, isn't it?" said Weatherby. "Now, if you don't mind, I have several new awards to tell the boys about and certificates to show them. We'll be handing them out after every game and every practice."

"Suits me," said Gus, "but doesn't having a bunch of awards lessen the impact? Won't the boys just start to throw the awards away?"

"We're nowhere near that level," said Weatherby as she reached into her large handbag and pulled out a bundle of new certificates. "You print their names on these and sign them, and I guarantee these boys will still have them when they're your age. I have my third-place ribbon from my first-grade relay team. That's all the more remarkable because there were only three teams in the race."

"I have a drawerful of proficiency badges from Cub Scouts," admitted Milt. "I have so many of them, I must have earned one every two weeks."

Alan said, "Well, then, let's go find some alignment and do a little repeated reward and recognition of our own."

When Weatherby introduced her awards, it turned out that she had three for each practice and game. There was the most improved award, the team spirit award, and the coach's choice award. The sparkle in the boys' eyes proved that the awards were going to be popular.

When Alan first started helping at hockey practice, he had taken turns with Milt and Gus working with the team. Now Weatherby had all three of them out on the ice full time and with specific instructions: no negative feedback.

"You can point out areas where they can improve and help them do better. That's your job. But don't nag them or criticize."

"I know I seem like the resident curmudgeon, but I think boys this age respond to a sharp word," said Gus.

"If they're rowdy, fighting, or that kind of thing, perhaps. Sometimes you have to get people's attention. And there have to be consequences for behavior. But what we're talking about here is building individual and team skills and knowledge. That's a very different thing.

"Ever been to Sea World, Gus?" she asked.

"I have."

"Like the show?"

"It was fantastic. They had a killer whale that could do anything! He played ball with the trainer and jumped over ropes. He even solved math problems and then counted out the answer by banging his flipper on the water."

"Do you know that those trainers do all that using only positive reinforcement?"

"You're kidding!"

"Think about it, Gus," said Weatherby. "Would you want to punish a killer whale for making a mistake and then get into the water with thousands of pounds of angry muscle and teeth?"

"No way," said Gus.

"If the Sea World trainers can send killer whales soaring into the air by accentuating the positive, then, doing the same, I think we should be able to train ten-year-old boys to put a puck into a net with no problem."

It was difficult to argue with Weatherby's reasoning, so the three of them were out on the ice seeking areas where what the boys were doing aligned with what they were working on. Then, they linked their praising to suggestions as to how they might be even better.

At the end of practice three award certificates were handed out. After seeing how thrilled the winners were, Alan had no trouble believing those pieces of paper would remain treasured possessions for a lifetime.

As the boys headed to the locker room, Weatherby called the coaching team together.

"Between practices I have lots of time to think about the boys and the four keys to building a high-five team," she said. "I've always liked to use word games or acronyms in my teaching. They help people remember. I've come up with one related to hockey and the four keys that I hope you'll find useful. It's an acronym based on the word 'puck.'"

"Let's hear it," said Milt.

"All right. The *P* stands for *providing* a clear purpose and shared values and goals. The *U* for *unleashing* and developing skills. The *C* is *creating* team power—none of us is as smart as all of us. The *K* is *keeping* the accent on the positive, my three R's—repeated reward and recognition."

"That does fit well," said Gus. "Providing, unleashing, creating, and keeping. Then purpose, skills, team power, and positive focus. Even I can remember that."

While driving Weatherby home that night, Alan said, "I've noticed that while we set winning the division cup as our big overall goal—our Holy Grail—you rarely talk about winning anything—even a game. Your focus is more on individual goals and skills and then translating that individual experience into team skills and knowledge. Even your three R's have us highlighting the personal skills and the resulting team skills."

Weatherby broke in: "You'd better let me talk, or I'll fall asleep on you. You're right. I want these boys to achieve personal bests and experience the magic of being part of a successful team, a high-five team, by doing things together they could never do on their own. Along the way they'll win some games, far more games than they'd win if they didn't use the four keys to successful teams.

"Winning is nice, Alan, but that's the by-product of building a great team. That's what we have to concentrate on."

Alan said, "I wondered if it had something to do with their being kids. If they were adults, would you talk about winning more?"

"I might, but I really shouldn't. If if you believe winning is everything, then by definition when you lose, you're nothing. That's a pretty shallow life, Alan.

"The good news is that if you put winning into perspective, you discover that lots of other things are important, too—sometimes more important than winning."

Alan said, "Are you saying a team can lose a game and still be successful?"

"Of course. If you play a great game against a spectacular opponent and lose, and you're a team that believes winning is everything, you leave the game with nothing. But a team that puts winning in perspective will come away still fired up and ready to plunge back into practice. The players will be excited that they played like a high-five team and be eager to build even stronger personal and team skills and knowledge. A simple question, Alan: Which one of those two teams was the loser?

"Another simple question: Which one has the best chance of finishing first the next time or the time after that?"

Alan didn't bother to reply. The answer was obvious. Teams with a focus on personal and team bests, a focus on team skills and knowledge, were going to be the real winners whether or not they won every game.

"You're awake, Weatherby?"

"I am."

"I want to tell you, it's fun handing out praise and linking that praise to things done right, rather than being critical and getting after the boys for making mistakes."

"I know the feeling," said Weatherby. "I know coaching is more fun this way—a lot more fun.

"The first year I coached basketball I was a screamer and a yeller. That's what all the other coaches were doing, and I started out following their lead. The girls paid attention if I got angry and yelled, so it seemed reasonable that if I wanted more from them, I should get angrier and yell louder."

"I can't imagine you doing that," said Alan.

"I don't like to remember what a jerk I was, but it's true."

"So what changed? Why did you change?"

"I was walking down the hall, and Miss Lane, our principal, was having a screaming fit at a pupil. She wound up pinching the child's cheek and using it to shake his head. Today that wouldn't happen, but this was forty years ago. It wasn't unusual behavior for her, but that day it suddenly occurred to me how wrong it was. Half of me was horrified at what she was doing to that child, and the other half wanted to laugh at what a total fool she was making of herself. I walked over, pulled her away from the student, and quietly told her to go to her office and calm down."

"What happened?" Alan asked when Weatherby fell silent.

"She didn't go to her office, that's for sure. She started to yell at me. I told her I wished I had a mirror to show her how silly she looked. She didn't care for the word 'silly,'" Weatherby said with a laugh. "It seems funny now, but it was pretty intense then. You know, I never saw her be abusive to another child, but that spring she took early retirement.

"The incident was so traumatic for me that I swore I'd never allow myself to do something stupid like that. I changed my coaching philosophy. It was easy because I'd never used the angry or yelling style in the classroom. I'd always been a believer in praise and gentle redirection when teaching. It worked for me as a teacher, and it started to work for me as a coach."

"I'm glad you made the switch," said Alan. "Tomorrow morning I'm off to sell all this to Mr. Monterro's company, and I'm going to give you half the fee—that is, if they decide I'm worth it and pay me."

"You'll be worth it, Alan. One thing I can spot are bright, good teachers. You'll be perfect. But I don't want any money. Jack and I have more than we can ever possibly use and no children. Nieces, nephews, and our main beneficiary, the United Way, are going to have quite a party when we die. But thank you for offering."

"I didn't mean . . ." Alan began.

"I know you didn't, but you have reminded me of something I've been wanting to say. I've been preaching teamwork at you, and yet I have not really treated you with the respect due a fellow team member."

"But you have," protested Alan.

"Let me finish. I have not given you or Milt or Gus the chance to really participate in deciding what the coaching team was going to do, or even how we were going to do it. I haven't guided our coaching team in how to reach coaching decisions. I've told you what to do, when to do it, and how to do it. That's hardly team building."

"We've been pretty directive with the boys, too," said Alan thoughtfully, thereby acknowledging Weatherby's point.

"There's a reason," said Weatherby. "When you came to see me, you had set yourself a near impossible task, winning the division cup. If I was going to help, I had to step in and be directive. It wasn't appropriate for me to start holding a series of coaching clinics over a six-month period the way I used to do for basketball coaches. It's much the same with the boys. They need firm direction—at least so far they do."

Alan and Weatherby drove for a minute before Weatherby spoke again.

"While it's appropriate for a leader to be directive when there is a crisis situation and the leader has special knowledge or skills that the team doesn't have, there comes a time when the leader has to back off and let the team become performers. We're reaching that point with our coaching team, Alan, and we'll need to start letting the boys take on more responsibility for strategy and direction soon. We won't give grade-five boys the scope we'd give a team of adults. They don't have the experiences and interpersonal skills to handle it. But we do have to let them move more in that direction."

They drove in silence while Alan thought about what Weatherby had said.

"Park Manor Home next stop," said Alan as he pulled into the driveway.

"Twice in a row you've made me miss my beauty rest," said Weatherby. "Your fault if I get wrinkles."

CHAPTER 12

As Alan made his final preparations for the session with Mr. Monterro and his company, he realized that the acronym P.U.C.K., while great for the boys hockey team, might not fit as well in a business presentation. In thinking about how he might organize the four keys for his new audience, the word "perform" came to mind. When he started to focus on it, everything he had learned from Weatherby fell into place. He saw the word "perform" as an acronym that covered it all. A high-performing team, a high-five team, would have the following characteristics:

P urpose and Values
E mpowerment
R elationships and Communications
F lexibility
O ptimal Performance
R ecognition and Appreciation
M orale

As he looked at his new acronym, Alan was pleased. P.E.R.F.O.R.M. recognized that the by-products of building a great team were optimal performance, (winning), and good morale—members were excited about being part of the team. To get high performance and high morale required *providing a clear purpose with shared values and goals, unleashing and developing skills* (empowerment and flexibility), *creating team power* (relationships and communication), and *keeping the accent on the positive* (recognition and appreciation).

Alan found giving a talk on teamwork a lot easier and more fun than he had expected. He shared the P.E.R.F.O.R.M. acronym along with what he had learned from Weatherby and his experience with the boys hockey team. He also poked fun at his own "puck hogging" behavior in the past. He ended the session where he had started by declaring that *none of us is as smart as all of us.*

Alan's presentation was inspiring. Just as Weatherby had predicted.

Mr. Monterro led a standing ovation. Alan hadn't pretended to know more than he knew, but what he did know he had presented with enthusiasm. He illustrated each point with stories, including ones from his own business career. But the stories the audience seemed to appreciate the most were his experiences as a coach with the Riverbend Warriors.

"Alan, you've made a difference," Mr. Monterro said as they walked to the exit door. "Your message is exactly what we needed. You've started us on a new journey. Here's your check. While all those people were crowded around you after your talk, I went back to my office and cut a new check. It's twice what I said I'd pay you, and I still think I've received far more than I'm paying for."

The last time Alan had been ushered out the door to a company parking lot, he hadn't been a happy man. This time he was grinning from ear to ear. When he showed the check to Susan, she said, "Well, genius, I think you've discovered your new career."

Alan's new career began that evening with three phone calls. Mr. Monterro had gone to a Rotary Club lunch and sung Alan's praises. He gave Alan's number out to several people. Best of all, he quoted the fee he had paid him and told people they'd better sign him up fast before Alan discovered what he was really worth.

Susan answered the first call while Alan was out at the store. She went ahead and made the booking. When Alan returned, they decided that Susan would become his manager, so she took the next two calls as well.

The next call was from George Burton, Alan's former employer. Burton obviously hadn't made the connection. Susan had decided that Alan needed a business name, and when the phone rang the third time, she created "Foster Performance Management" on the spot.

"I hear Mr. Foster is a teamwork expert," said Mr. Burton. "I'm a big believer in teamwork, and Alec Monterro gives him rave reviews. I'd like to have Mr. Foster give the keynote address at our annual Week of Excellence."

Susan was so stunned that she wasn't sure what to do, so she took the booking. It was several months off. Alan could think about it and there was still plenty of time for Mr. Burton to book someone else if Alan didn't want to do it.

"Not do it! Of course I want to do it," said Alan after Susan hung up the phone. "We'll get some stationery, write confirmation letters, and offer a money-back guarantee. Then when Burton finds out it's me, he won't have to pay if he doesn't want to."

"As long as you're comfortable," said Susan.

"I am. I know that company inside out, and I now know something about teamwork. I really believe I can be helpful."

The next day was Thursday, a practice day. That afternoon Alan picked up his son, David, from school as he usually did now. He enjoyed picking up David, and at the same time he got the homework assignments for Tim and then dropped them off at his house on the way home. It was a task he'd undertaken when he realized that the hours Tim's dad worked prevented him from doing so.

When Alan stopped by with Tim's homework on days when his dad was home, he usually stayed awhile to chat. In the process he was able to learn something about Wes Burrows's background.

"When Sandra died, I just wanted to run, keep on the move. I was human resources manager for a large plant in town, and I couldn't bear going into the office, so I quit and moved here. The house we'd lived in as a family was too full of ghosts. When we got here, I needed a job. Whatever savings I'd had went to pay Sandra's medical bills that were not covered by our insurance. But I didn't want a job where I had to bring problems home. I needed something where every day was complete and nothing carried over to the next day. Being a waiter has been perfect except for the hours. Every time you turn a table, the job is complete. There's lots to keep you busy, keep you on your toes, but you get closure constantly."

It was Wes Burrows's next words that Alan remembered now as he and David rang Tim's doorbell. "I've been thinking lately that I'm about ready to go out and get a business job again. At one time I did a lot of training. I liked that, and I was good at it. Perhaps I'll try that again."

The door opened.

"Hello, Mr. Foster. Hi, David. Homework, I bet."

"That's right, Tim. Glad to see you back home."

"Yeah. The tests were fine. Just an ordinary nosebleed. I can go back to school in a day or two."

"That's great. I'm glad to see you don't need those crutches anymore. Your dad's off from work today, isn't he? Is he here?"

"Dad," Tim bellowed. "Mr. Foster's here." Then he added, "Hey, David, wanna see the neat train my aunt sent me?"

The boys ran off, and Alan Foster had lots of time to present his ideas for Burrows Foster Performance Management, Inc., to Tim's father.

When he called to David that it was time to go, Alan had a partner. Wes Burrows had agreed to everything except the name. The new firm would be Foster Burrows, not Burrows Foster.

CHAPTER 13

The Thursday practice was a great success, but not as successful as the game on Saturday.

The boys won against one of the best teams in the league. It was considered a good team because it had two star players who scored all the goals. But they didn't have teamwork, and they didn't have any plan to defend themselves against a team that did. It was close, but the final score was Riverbend Warriors, 5; Hillside Tigers, 4.

Weatherby again didn't attend. Tim was in the stands, and to the surprise of Milt, Gus, and Alan, so was Mr. Boothe, Jed's father. After the game he came over and said, "You're working magic with those boys. You're teaching them teamwork. It's incredible. I don't want my Jed to miss out on this. He'll be at practice on Tuesday."

The three coaches gave one another nervous looks. Finally, Milt spoke. "We've been doing some things differently. Working plays. Passing."

"And you're worried about Jed's fitting in, right?"

"I'm not sure 'fitting in' is exactly the concern," said Alan, wondering what he should say, if anything.

"Look. The problem with Jed is that he's a puck hog," said Mr. Boothe, to everyone's surprise. "He happens to be six or eight months ahead of the others on growth, so he has a bit more size and better coordination. That isn't going to last. He needs to learn to be a team player, or he's never going to go very far in life. That's why I want him back here. This may even be as important as schoolwork."

"We'll be delighted to see him on Tuesday," said Milt.

"I'll tell him that you've made some changes and explain to him that he has to adapt to the new system. You'll have all my support," said Mr. Boothe.

When Alan phoned Weatherby with the score and the news that Jed was coming back, she said, "Another week would have been nice, but the support of his father more than makes up for that."

"You're not worried the boys need more time?" asked Alan.

"We'll be fine. Jed will do well, too, provided we get his goals for practice and games agreed on. Then whenever we catch him aligned with what we're working on—purpose, skills, or synergetic harmony—we'll load on repeated rewards and recognition."

Weatherby was right. With the support of Mr. Boothe, Jed arrived at practice delighted to be back early and open to learning teamwork. The boys were excited to see him back, and the coaches found lots of opportunity to give him positive feedback. Whatever his dad had told him, it was working. Jed was actually eager to coordinate his play with the rest of the team. He won that day's coach's choice award. His willingness to pass and be part of a planned play won great praise during the presentation.

"Jed's going to fit right in. He'll raise the level of our team skills and challenge others. Come Saturday we'll really be a high-five team," said Weatherby on the ride home. "A high-performing person who is also a team player will raise the level of everyone else. The team will play up, rather than the high performer playing down." It was the only thing she said. Her pronouncement made, she fell asleep.

Two nights later, on the way home from Thursday practice, Alan again asked if he could pick her up for the game on Saturday. For the first time Weatherby told Alan why she never went to games.

"Saturday is dance night," she said. "They play music and we dance. Afterward we have hot cocoa and cake. It's not very different from the dances I went to as a teenager. Even much of the music is the same."

Alan was about to comment when Weatherby continued, "Saturday night makes going to games tough. On dance night Jack is more alive and closer to the Jack I married than on any other night of the week. It's also the only time I get held, Alan. We don't have many Saturday nights left. Each one is precious."

Alan reached over and gave Weatherby's arthritic hand a gentle squeeze. They completed the trip in silence. Weatherby didn't sleep.

Tim wasn't sleeping, either. He was sitting at the window of his darkened room, looking out into the night sky, and having a heart-to-heart talk with his mother. He had survived the accident. He hated missing hockey, but he knew he would survive that provided he could go back. When the doctors said he could play again next year, he accepted that as being the case. He'd play again next year. Now he wasn't so sure.

"Everything's changing, Mom. Since the accident Coach Foster has this lady, Weatherby, helping. Remember, I told you about her? Well, they're changing everything, and everybody is getting so good, I'm worried I'll get left behind."

After a few minutes of silence Tim said, "Good night, Mom," blew a kiss out to the dark night sky, and went to bed.

Mom must have been listening.

As Weatherby walked up to the Park Manor door with Alan, she spoke for the first time since telling him of dance night.

"We have one loose end, Alan—this boy Tim who hurt himself. I keep thinking about him. I know you're starting to work with his dad, but from what you say, it will be at least a few months before he can quit his restaurant job. Until then, that boy is home alone and needs help. He's part of the team. He's our responsibility."

"What do you suggest we do?"

"I don't know. Are you sure he can't play? I had a girl break a bone in her foot once. They said she couldn't play, but then her parents had a special brace made and she was able to play some."

"That might do for Tim, too. I guess we have to find out," said Alan.

"Who is his doctor?"

"I don't know who his own doctor is, but I met the surgeon. She's wonderful. Her name is Nancy Cantor."

"Nancy Cantor! I taught a Nancy Cantor. Who knows? It may be the same one. She was going into medicine. I'll get on it in the morning."

It was the same Nancy Cantor, and she had a good reason for not giving all the options to Tim's father.

"His insurance wouldn't cover it, and I know he's struggling to make ends meet. The special helmet and neck brace would be at least twenty-five hundred dollars. That father has enough sadness in his life without knowing that if he had the money, his son could play."

"The boy would be safe if he had this helmet and neck brace? You're sure?"

"Nothing is *sure,* but I can tell you that with the equipment he'd be the least likely boy on the team to sustain that type of injury. It's just too bad that his dad doesn't have that kind of money."

He didn't, but Weatherby did. Two hours later Nancy Cantor was on the phone to Tim's father, telling him that Tim had been accepted into a special grant program which would supply a helmet and neck brace at no charge. Tim didn't play Saturday, but he was scheduled to practice with the team the next week and play the following Saturday. As he walked home after the game, he knew somehow, once again, Mom had taken care of things. He left the arena so fast that no one had a chance to offer him a ride. He needed time to say thanks.

The helmet and brace were ready for Thursday. For the first time in weeks Tim was on the ice, ready to practice with the team. And never had he been better equipped to practice. To his amazement, and his father's, the program that Dr. Cantor was working with also provided new skates, a new stick, and a full set of shoulder, knee, and elbow pads. Tim's letter of thanks to the fund's trustees had been hand-delivered by Nancy Cantor, and using her computer she'd created some wonderful stationery on which the fund's executive director—also instantly created—wrote Tim back, wishing him well.

Tim skated slowly around the ice, getting used to the feel of being on skates again, and he marveled at his new equipment. Mom might not answer every time he called on her, but when she did . . . !

Over in the coach's box Alan turned to Weatherby and said, "Some coincidence, isn't it? I give you Nancy Cantor's name, and the next day she's on the phone to Tim's dad with the most incredible grant program."

Weatherby smiled.

"You really are amazing," said Alan quietly. "But I can't say that I'm surprised. When Milt asked me if you had any children, I told him you had more kids than anyone else I knew."

"I like to think so, Alan. I like to think so."

The moment was shattered by a blast from Coach Gorman's whistle. Coaches and boys alike headed for center ice and the start of practice. Jed and Tim were back. The Riverbend Warriors were again at full strength and ready to play high-five hockey.

CHAPTER 14

Early on, after listening to the Riverbend Warriors' chant, other coaches hadn't hesitated to take some good-natured digs at Milt, Gus, and Alan. On the ice their teams had laughed at the Riverbend players. And why not? No one saw the perennially cellar-dwelling Warriors as potential contenders for the division cup.

By midseason the jests and jeers had died down. As the season drew to a close, other teams groaned when they learned that their next game would be against Riverbend, while their coaches began seeking advice from Milt, Gus, and Alan. One coach they didn't consult was Weatherby. She never attended games, and when Riverbend coaches and team members alike stuck to the story of an ancient African-American lady who lived in a nursing home as the source of their success, all concluded this was an elaborately concocted tale to hide whoever was really behind Riverbend's success.

Numerous stories made the rounds. Several involved a National Hockey League coach. Some said he was being paid. Some said he was an uncle of one of the Riverbend boys. No one believed the lady in the nursing home story.

Bud Benson, coach of the Sandy Point Winterhawks, a team that usually dwelt in the cellar with the Riverbend Warriors, went so far as to drop by a Riverbend practice.

"Hi, Milt. I was in the area and remembered that you practiced on Thursdays, so I thought I'd drop in and say hello."

"Good to see you, Bud. It gives us a chance to introduce you to our secret weapon, Miss Weatherby," said Milt, sure that that was why Bud happened to be in the neighborhood.

Weatherby uncharacteristically mumbled her hello and then, leaning close to Bud's face, said, "You want a hamburger? They always get me a hamburger." Turning away, she abruptly sat down and began to pick at a button on her coat, mumbling to herself and ignoring Milt and Bud.

Embarrassed, Milt stammered something to Bud about Weatherby's not quite being herself. Minutes later Bud departed, with one last glance at Weatherby who continued to sit with her head down, picking at her button.

From the corner of her eye, Weatherby watched Bud depart and then looked up at Milt with a huge smile.

"What are you doing?" said Milt.

"Driving 'em nuts," said Weatherby with a burst of laughter. "You don't suppose Bud just happened by, do you? Now let's get out there and get these boys ready to play high-five hockey on Saturday. "

When Bud got home, he telephoned several other coaches. The message to them all was the same: Riverbend was up to something so secret that they'd even hired an old lady from a nursing home to help with the cover-up.

Weatherby's first game was the season's last. She didn't sit with the other coaches, though. She had Jack with her, and the two sat in reserved seats right behind the players' bench. Normally, reserved seats weren't needed, but this game was a sudden-death final and the winner would go home with the division cup. The arena was packed. Riverbend had made it to the cup. Thirty minutes of hockey, three ten-minute periods, would determine the winner.

For the first time anyone could remember, newspaper reporters and television news crews were in attendance. Riverbend's road from the cellar to the top of the league was the kind of human-interest story sportscasters and writers loved.

The novelty of the media presence was of more interest to the parents and other spectators than it was to the Riverbend team, which burst onto the ice one last time, chanting:

Pum Nim, Kat Nim
This Is Our Pledge To Tim.
Keemo, Kimo, Derrah, Stamps,
Riverbend Will Be The Champs.
Wear Ah, Tare Ah, Tanie Gleem,
Warriors Are A High-Five Team.

"Well, Weatherby, are we going to win?" asked Alan, leaning back over the wooden rail that separated Weatherby's seats from the players' box.

"We already have," said Weatherby. "Every one of those boys has experienced the magic of being part of a high-five team. It's a lesson they'll never forget."

"You're right about that," said Alan. "Having a good time, sir?" he added, turning to Jack.

"The best. I haven't been to a hockey game in years."

Weatherby looked at Jack in surprise. On the way out of the nursing home that evening she'd whispered to Alan that Jack was having a good day. It was difficult for Alan to tell. Jack had been silent during the whole trip and had given no indication that he knew where they were going.

"Only trouble with school games instead of professional ones is you get hot chocolate instead of beer," Jack added with a laugh as he lifted his Styrofoam cup of hot chocolate in mock salute.

Alan turned back to the ice, pretending he hadn't noticed the tear sliding down Weatherby's cheek as she reached over and held on to Jack's free hand.

As the boys skated through the warmup routine, Alan focused his attention on the opposition. He felt that a good tip-off to a game's final outcome came from observing the opposition coaches before the action started. The louder they yelled, the more they shouted orders, the more they berated boys for making errors—all common coaching techniques—the more likely it was that Riverbend would win.

Today, though, the signs were not good. The Meadowland Thunderjets were team players led by coaches whose philosophy closely matched that of Alan, Milt, and Gus. Before the game the Meadowland head coach, Bob Pasternac, had gone to the Riverbend dressing room and offered a proposal to Milt. "I know you're a believer in teamwork, and you've done a great job with these boys. I hope I've done half as well with mine. I'd like to make a proposition. Before and after the game let's defy the league governors and have the boys shake hands in a skate-past at center ice." It took Milt less than a millisecond to agree.

Each team had been briefed, and when the warmup skate had ended, Alan shuffled out to mid-ice with Milt and Gus. The coaches would lead their teams through the handshake skate-past. Moments later each team lined up behind its coaching staff, and to the astonishment of the game officials, who had just come on the ice, they began to skate alongside each other, exchanging greetings, best wishes, and handshakes.

The head referee skated over and said to the coaches in a voice loud enough for the players and parents to hear, "Congratulations! It's good to see sportsmanship back on the ice."

The head referee wasn't the only one handing out compliments, and for Alan that was another bad sign as to the final outcome.

From the moment the Meadowland Thunderjets hit the ice for their warmup skate, their coaches were calling out encouragement and praise from the bench. Alan thought he, Milt, and Gus had become adept at spotting the boys doing things right and then handing out rewards and recognition, but he had to admit these other coaches were their equal. And the coaches had apparently worked with the same group of boys in grades three and four as well as this year.

Because of the way the various sections within the division were scheduled during the season, this would be the first time the Riverbend Warriors and the Meadowland Thunderjets met on ice. From the opening whistle it was obvious the two teams were evenly matched. By the end of the first period the score was tied one goal apiece. At the end of the second, Riverbend led 2 to 1. At the end of the third period the score was tied 3 to 3.

The teams played two five-minute sudden-death periods with no change in the score. By then both sides were exhausted. As the kids sat on the bench to catch their breath, the head referee called the coaches to center ice and said, "We've never had a situation like this before, so you may be unaware that the league rules state if the game is still tied after two overtime periods, the gold goes to the team with the best win/loss record during the regular season."

The coaches knew their records. Riverbend had two more losses. The Meadowland Thunderjets would be awarded the cup. The Riverbend Warriors would be the silver medal winners.

Milt had the sad task of returning from center ice to tell the boys the bad news. It was made easier by Bob Pasternac. "I'll wait here and chat with the ref while you go over and tell your team. It's best they hear it from you rather than from my bunch cheering. Then if they're up to it, I'd still like to do a handshake skate-past."

The Riverbend Warriors gathered around Milt to hear the news.

"It turns out we don't get to play a third overtime. The championship gets decided on which team has the season's best win/loss record," Milt said. He paused. He could tell from the looks that the boys knew exactly what that meant. It was just as well he didn't have to speak the words. The lump of disappointment in his throat threatened to choke off anything he might try to say. His disappointment was for the boys, not for himself. They had worked so hard, they had come so close, and now to lose . . .

"But we're undefeated!" whooped Tim. "We made it to the division cup, and we're undefeated in the sudden death final. We get undefeated silver." Suddenly Tim's teammates joined in with such enthusiasm that you'd have thought they won. In fact, Bob Pasternac reported later, that was exactly what his boys thought had happened because they hadn't yet heard from him.

Milt laughed and, turning to Alan and Gus, said, "I swear if that boy woke up on Christmas morning and found a pile of horse manure under the Christmas tree, he'd go running around the house looking for a pony."

The Riverbend team banged their sticks and threw helmets and gloves in the air in joyous celebration of being undefeated in the division cup final. On the other side of the ice similar pandemonium engulfed the Meadowland Thunderjets, and it was several minutes before the coaches could get their teams lined up to skate past and shake hands.

After the game the Riverbend Warriors adjourned to McDonald's along with Weatherby and Jack, who seemed as bright as he had before the game. "No wonder," said Weatherby when Alan mentioned it. "After you spoke to him, he dozed off until the middle of the third period."

"Look at him now, though," said Alan. Two tables over, Jack was sitting with a group of boys and telling them stories. "He's doing great."

"He is. Until you rescued me, I hadn't realized how much I missed the stimulation of being around children. I completely ignored the fact that Jack's world was deadly dull, too. I knew it, of course, but I just failed to recognize that he could still respond to others."

"You'll bring him to the awards banquet then? Two weeks from Friday?"

"We'll go," said Weatherby. "But isn't that your big day at your old company?"

"I meet with them at two o'clock. Same time of day and same day of the week that I was fired."

"George Burton will want you back. If he doesn't, he's crazy—but not as crazy as you if you do go back. I'll be at the dinner, that's for sure, and I'll want a full report."

CHAPTER 15

On the day of the division cup banquet every member of the Riverbend team and coaching staff, save one, bounded out of bed eager for the evening banquet. The exception was Alan Foster. Before he could attend the banquet, he had to pay a visit to his former company. What had seemed like such a good idea now seemed like anything but.

Foster Burrows Performance Management had rented a small office, and when Alan arrived, Wes Burrows was already there with the coffee brewing. The demand for Alan's services had been so great that Wes joined him earlier than either had anticipated.

Wes's previous experience in training and as a human resource manager for a large company was invaluable. Alan had been concerned that lack of formal training and certification would hamper their efforts to be effective in the field, but he quickly found out that wasn't the case. His audiences immediately recognized the power of the four keys Weatherby had given him for building a high-five team. As he poured himself a coffee, Alan quickly ran through the P.U.C.K. acronym in his mind.

First, **providing** a clear sense of purpose with values and goals, reinforced with a charter or a covenant that gave team members a reason to trade self for selflessness.

Second, **unleashing** and developing skills—continuously building individual skills that, in turn, bolstered collective skills. Alan was still in awe of the fact that the team itself had built a collective skill level which transcended the individual skills so much that even if a highly skilled player dropped out, the team continued at a high level. Team skills were more than the sum of individual skills. Alan had seen this happen when Jed, the team's most skilled player, was sick with the flu and couldn't make an important game three weeks after he had returned to the team. He was missed, but they still squeaked out a win against a tough opponent. Rather than falling apart, as they would have in the first weeks of the season, they played together, covering, passing, and keeping control of the puck.

Third, **creating** team power. "None of us is as smart as all of us" had been the real turning point. Alan also liked the phrase's synergistic harmony. The boys might not understand the words, but they knew exactly what Coach Foster meant. They realized that by working together as a team they could beat the best there is, if the best there is didn't work as a team. This realization had convinced everyone that the Holy Grail of the division cup really could be theirs. The other teams had larger, more skilled players but very little teamwork.

Fourth, **keeping** the accent on the positive—Weatherby's three R's, repeated reward and recognition—had, as she promised, closed the loop to the other three keys. The coaches had deliberately sought instances where behavior was aligned with efforts in those areas. The age-old wisdom that people repeat performance for which they get praised turned out to be right on for grade-five boys. Praise was acknowledged with big grins and dedication to doing even better.

While Alan was convinced of the power of what he had learned from Weatherby, he confessed to his partner: "I don't mind telling you, Wes, I'm worried about this assignment. George Burton may throw a fit when he sees me."

As he so often did, Wes put the matter in perspective. "What's the worst that can happen? Is Burton going to fire you again? Go in there, man. Stand tall. Think big. Act big. Be big. You're going to be a sensation, same as always."

For moral support that afternoon Wes accompanied Alan. "What are you muttering?" Wes asked as they walked up to the company's front entrance.

"Stand tall. Think big. Act big. Be big," said Alan. "Just remembering your advice."

Fortunately for Alan, George Burton wasn't at the door to meet him. Allison Preston, who did greet him, was new since Alan's time and brought Mr. Burton's apologies. He'd be a few minutes late.

Alan followed Allison to the stage of the auditorium without incident, but once on the platform, most of the people in the room recognized him as he stood slightly to the side while Allison again expressed Burton's regrets for being late. She then read a glowing introduction, which she revealed had been written by the president himself. Allison had practiced her presentation and thought she'd done a good job, but after she finished the audience sat in stunned silence. Somehow this had to be a colossal April Fools joke. The month was right, but it wasn't the first. The silence continued as Alan walked to center stage.

"Good morning, friends and former associates. It's good to be back. As you can tell from the introduction, I've taken up a new career since I last saw you," Alan began bravely, then thudded to a halt as George Burton entered at the back of the room. Most of the audience looked over their shoulders to see what had caused Alan to stop so abruptly. What they saw was their president gaping and speechless.

"Before I begin my presentation today, I'd like to say a few words about Mr. Burton." Alan's voice floated out over the heads that immediately snapped back to face him. The seven hundred employees all had the same thought: it's going to hit the fan! This was followed by a second: I wouldn't miss this for the world.

"In the past few months I've had the opportunity to visit many different companies and organizations, and I've met a number of presidents and had the chance to assess them," continued Alan as his audience edged to the front of their chairs in anticipation of the bombshell about to drop.

"I can tell you that this company is darn lucky to be led by Mr. Burton. He has energy, drive, and vision. He has had the guts to clean out some deadwood that needed cleaning out—deadwood that should have been dealt with long before he came here. When you cut deadwood from a tree, the tree is healthier. Sometimes even the deadwood benefits. My grandmother once told me about the Appaloosa tree. When wood falls from the Appaloosa tree, she said, it begins to root, and soon a fresh, new tree springs up." Alan paused and looked out over the audience before adding, "I must be Appaloosa."

From the back of the auditorium came the sound of one person clapping enthusiastically. The audience turned again. It was Mr. Burton clapping. Others joined in what became thunderous applause.

You should have heard him," Wes said to Weatherby at the banquet that evening. "Alan gave an inspired presentation. George Burton, the one who had him fired, led a standing ovation when he was finished. He wants Alan to come back to work for him."

Weatherby wheeled on Alan. "You're not going to, are you?"

"I am."

"You're crazy. I warned you," said Weatherby.

"Sorry, but it was just too good an offer to pass up."

Weatherby looked at Alan with fire in her eyes. "Now listen to me, Alan Foster. I sure hope you haven't signed any sort of contract yet."

"Well, I haven't yet, but I will. It's a great consulting contract. Wes and I will be there one day every two weeks for the next year, and the money is fantastic," said Alan. And then he grinned at Weatherby and said, "Got you!"

Weatherby gave Alan a smile back. If it had been seen by Jack, he could have told Alan that it meant Weatherby would get even sometime!

The highlight of the evening was the presentation of the medals. The Riverbend Warriors were called to the front, and a silver-plated medal bearing their name and dangling from a red sash was hung around the neck of each player. The coaches, too, were awarded medals, and the loudest applause of the evening was for Weatherby as she accepted hers.

The only person not applauding, simply because he was too astounded to do so, was Bud Benson, coach of the Sandy Point Winterhawks, who had last seen Weatherby at a Riverbend practice calmly picking at a button.

On her way back to her seat Weatherby passed by where Bud was sitting. When she reached him, she stopped, leaned over, and said, "This sure beats the hamburger I usually get."

The evening quickly drew to a close. Alan, as always, drove Weatherby and Jack home, and on the way suggested his company name might sound better if it were Weatherby Foster Burrows. "You could come in a day or two a week for a few hours," said Alan. "I'd pick you up."

"No. I can't agree to that. But Foster Burrows Weatherby might work."

Tim rode home with his dad. As he climbed into the car, he had a special request. "I'd like to drive out by the edge of town on the way home, if that's okay—you know, out at the end of Four Mile Road."

"Sure, but why out there?"

"Kinda reminds me of where we used to live."

"And Mom?"

After a long pause Tim said, "Yeah, and Mom."

"It's dark. Wouldn't you rather go tomorrow?"

"No. Tonight, please. I don't mind the dark."

A few minutes later they reached the spot where Four Mile Road turned into State 508, beyond streetlights.

"Can we stop here for a minute, Dad? I'd like to get out by myself."

Tim's dad didn't know what it was all about, but he could tell it was important. He was sure Tim would be safe enough, so he pulled over onto the gravel shoulder and stopped.

Tim stepped into the cool night air of spring and walked slowly out into the newly ploughed cornfield that ran alongside the road. Clouds covered the full moon, and it was pitch black. Just as Tim's dad lost sight of him and decided he should get out of the car, the clouds broke and a brilliant moon shone through to illuminate Tim. His dad settled back in his seat. If he'd been closer, he would have seen Tim's uplifted face.

"Thanks, Mom," Tim whispered to the moonbeams. "I'm glad I played hockey. And, Mom, you know what? Next year we're going to have a real high-five team. We're going to win the division cup."

Then Tim held up the silver-plated medal that hung around his neck as if to show it to the moon. "Look, Mom. Isn't this great? It's for you, Mom. It says:

"Timothy Albert Burrows
Riverbend Warriors
Team Member"

AFTERWORD

Each of us knows that the *High Five!* you've just read is a far, far better book than any one of us could have produced on his or her own. However, if it were up to us as individuals, each of us would handle some things differently.

Wrapped up in these observations is an important lesson. Where there is team magic, there may also be personal frustration or even pain. Being part of a productive High Five team doesn't mean taking your best stuff—and then cherry picking other team members' best stuff—to come up with your personal, unique view of a perfect product, plan, or program. The reality is that while you're cherry picking their stuff, they are cherry picking yours!

If you're going to be a part of a High Five team, you have to be willing to accept some losses. Fight for your ideas certainly. Try to convince others. But if they can't or won't buy in to your thinking, it's time to take a deep breath and let go. Another time, another project, another team, and your brilliant idea may be appreciated. This time, though, get your ego out of the way and move on. Learning to let go, to put the team's will first, is an empowering experience that leads to the most wonderful of all experiences: being a member of a high-performing, gung-ho, High Five team.

Writing this book has been a true team experience. Each of us has had specific responsibilities as well as overall responsibility for every page, paragraph, and sentence. If you learned half as much about teams from reading this book as we did while creating it, if you had half as much fun reading as we did writing it, if your next team experience is half as good as ours has been, then we will consider this project a High Five success.

None of us is as smart as all of us.

From all of us,
Ken Blanchard, Sheldon Bowles,
Don Carew, Eunice Parisi-Carew

PUTTING IT ALL TOGETHER

High Five! stands squarely on the shoulders of two previous books: *The One Minute Manager Builds High Performing Teams* and *Gung Ho!* that told readers how to turn on the people in any organization. Readers wanting to know more are encouraged to read those two books.

The One Minute Manager Builds High Performing Teams is primarily about process. It also focuses on the phases of team development and leadership behaviors that facilitate excellence. The P.E.R.F.O.R.M. acronym found in *High Five!* originated in the high-performing teams book and is discussed there in more detail.

Gung Ho! on the other hand, deals primarily with creating and focusing individual and group energy. The key concepts of *Gung Ho!* are: *Worthwhile Work, In Control of Achieving the Goal,* and *Cheering Each Other On.*

Readers of these two books have asked if they fit together, and if so, how? They do, and *High Five!* is also aligned. Indeed, it may be helpful to think of *High Five!* as a bridge between the two. For the benefit of trainers, team leaders, and interested team members the chart on the next page shows how all three books align and integrate. Then on the following page, you will find our High Five Team Soaring to Success Balloon, a graphic representation of the P.U.C.K. acronym that shows how repeated reward and recognition focused on aligned behavior is the magic that sends the team soaring to success.

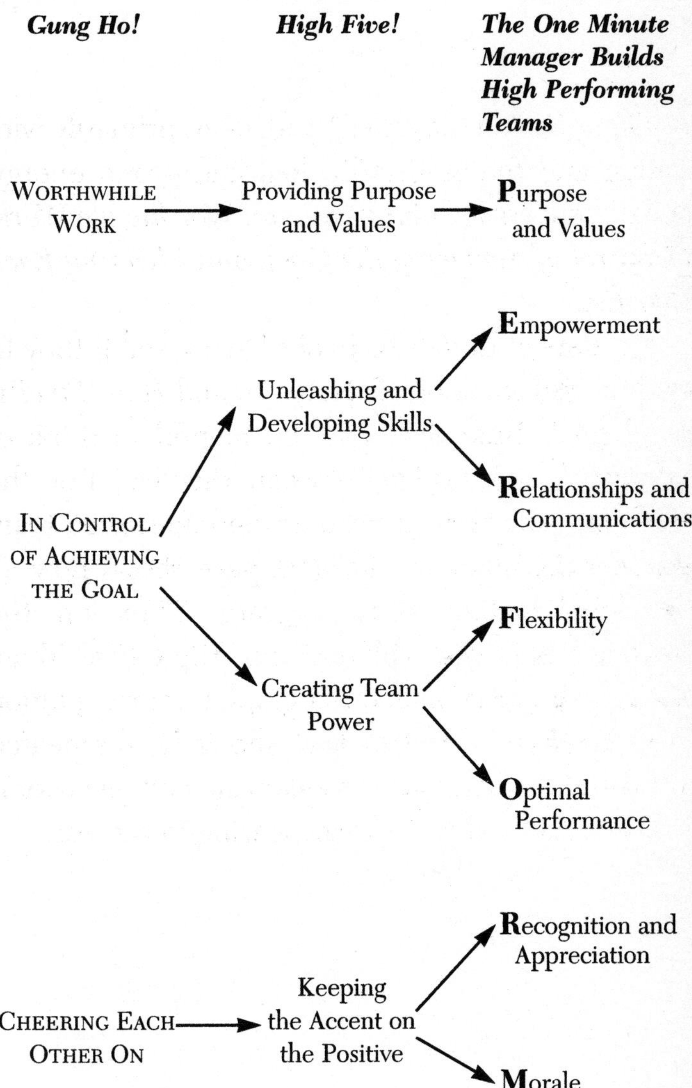

Gung Ho!
High Five!
The One Minute Manager Builds High Performing Teams
WORTHWHILE WORK
Providing Purpose and Values
Purpose and Values
Empowerment
Unleashing and Developing Skills
Relationships and Communications
IN CONTROL OF ACHIEVING THE GOAL
Flexibility
Creating Team Power
Optimal Performance
Recognition and Appreciation
Keeping the Accent on the Positive
CHEERING EACH OTHER ON
Morale

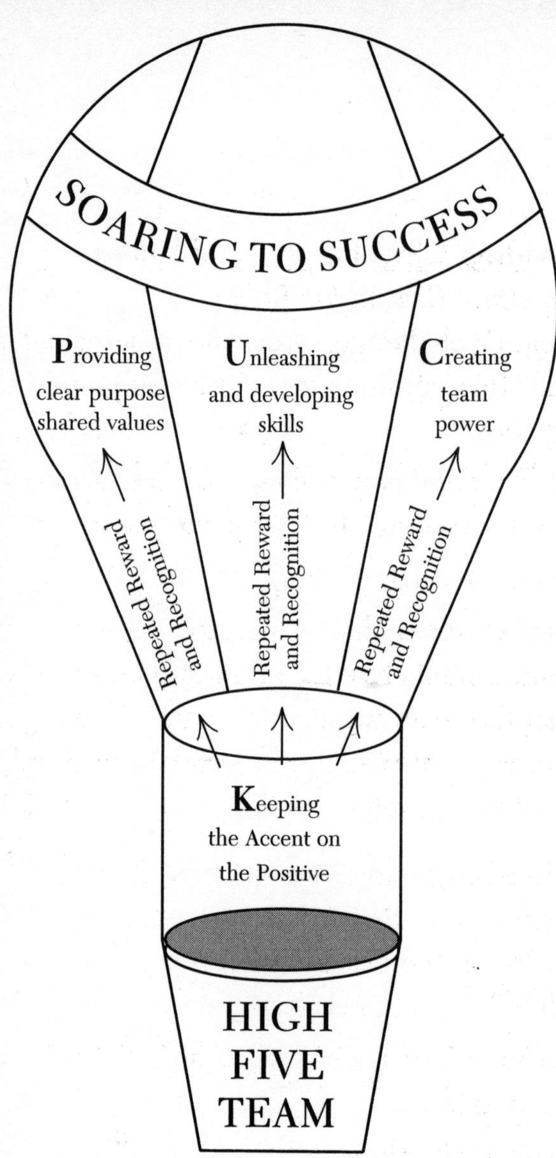

Repeated reward and recognition is more than blowing hot air. Accentuating the positive is the lift that sends teams soaring. Without it you'll be stuck on the ground.

P Providing Clear Purpose and Values

A Compelling Reason for Being

- Create a challenge, a reason for being, a "holy grail" that commits and motivates people to work together.
- Set clear and compelling goals and strategies, both for the individual and the team.
- Be clear on your values.
- Create a team charter that formalizes commitments to each other and clearly states what the team wants to accomplish, why it is important, and how the team will work together to achieve results.

U Unleashing and Developing Skills

Developing Your Bench Strength

- Start with the basics. Build individual skills that will bolster team skills.
- Provide feedback to build skills, confidence, and accountability.
- Learn each other's roles.
- Build a sense of personal and collective power by using your individual and collective skills to achieve extraordinary results.

C Creating Team Power
None of us is as smart as all of us. Synergistic harmony.

- Build a game plan for the team and stick to it.
- Share leadership.
- Reward team work.
- Rotate positions to build flexibility, introduce change, and build mental and physical skills.
- Turn individual skills into team skills.

K Keeping the Accent on the Positive
Repeated Reward and Recognition

- Look for behaviors that reflect the purpose and values, skill development, and team work, and reward, reward, reward those behaviors.
- Catch people doing things right or approximately right.
- Redirect toward the goal; do not punish.
- Link all recognition and reward back to the purpose and goals.

GOOSE HONKINGS*

Books don't just happen. At least ours don't. From an idea to final book, countless colleagues, advisors, friends, and airline seatmates give us feedback, criticism, encouragement, and fresh insights. Among the many people who have helped us, we particularly want to thank:

Lisa Queen, a key member of our William Morrow High Five publishing team whose integrity, wisdom, warmth, and unfailing book sense has helped make the association with Morrow a pleasure, and writing books a joy.

Alan Snart, Western Management Consultants, a teamwork genius, whose keen eye and sharp insights are always welcome.

*Honking geese are cheering each other on, according to Andy Longclaw in our book *Gung Ho!*

Ken Hartwig, Jim DeSpain, Charlie Hughes, Ann Oliver, Rich Seeman, John Kerby, Steve Berry, Don Drake, Bob Gordon, Jerry Wright, Cleon Streitmatter, Ed Mallon, Caterpillar Track Type Tractors.

Charles and **Edith Seashore,** NTL Institute, who were early mentors and guides of experiential learning and team dynamics.

Rocco Ricci and **Mike Green,** Concord Hospital.

Hugh Goldie, Peter Wintemute, and all the rest of the High Five team at the Exchange Group, whose support and advice are much valued.

Scott Gassman and **Linda S. Gianni,** Empire Blue Cross Blue Shield.

Dwayne Reiser, Meyers Norris Penny, an integral part of the team that keeps Sheldon on track and productive.

Byron Diggs, Jimmy King, and **Tony Malafronte,** Guilford Fibers.

Brian Black, whose enthusiasm and help is much appreciated.

Rich Woodrome, Chris Burt, Barry Pickering, Willie Everett, Hills Pet Nutrition.

Bailey and **Rita Jackson,** University of Massachusetts, who taught Eunice the importance and value of diversity in a team setting.

Betty Blee, Ross Tartell, John Kamovitch, Rich Braaten, Ray Johnson, Julie Ellis, David Gensure, John Helman, David Knapp, Pfizer Pharmaceuticals.

Robert Cole, Certainteed, a great supporter of The Ken Blanchard Companies, who has allowed us to use Certainteed as a beta testing site for several products.

Howard Bickley and **Alan Greene,** Union Camp.

Kingsley A. Bowles, Sheldon's brother, who will recognize several places where his good advice has made *High Five!* a better book.

Jim Middleton, Dawn Quist-Harrington, Barnie Bunnell, Gloria French, Marcelina Gilliam, Larry Raines, Allied Signal.

Spencer Johnson, M.D., for his generous foreword, support, and wisdom.

Nancy Maher, **Bill Finneran**, **Kevin Ford**, **Frank DeSisto**, **Lisa O'Neill**, **Jim Brennerman**, **Joe DiRoberto**, **Steve Dunlap**, **Pete Mancuso**, **Paul Brunelle**, **Pete Lindenmeyer**, **Jeff Bruell**, **Kate McNally**, **Vince Hernandez**, T.J.Maxx.

John Dahl, **Jeanne Aandal**, and **Bill Friday**, whose High Five team at Canada Safeway in Kenora, Ontario, exemplifies what happens when Gung Ho team members deliver unfailing Raving Fan Service®—sales per square foot that lead the company!

Don sends his special thanks to his **Shagbark** family members who, over the years, have taught him so much about teams.

As always we are indebted to Sheldon's High Five YPO Forum team: **Richard Andison**, **David Baldner**, **Sheldon Berney**, **Trevor Cochrane**, **Carl Eisbrenner**, **Derek Johannson**, **Ray Kives**, **Richard Kroft**, **Mel Lazareck**, **Sam Linhart**, **Bob May**, **Michael Nozick**, **Maureen Prendiville**, **Hartley Richardson**, **Ross Robinson**, **Paul Schimnowski**, **Harvey Secter**, **Gary Steiman**, and **Jim Tennant**.

The manuscript of *High Five!* was read by some very special people who have been generous with their time and advice: **Senator Douglas D. Everett; Ed Chornous; Ray Moon; Paul Petrick** and **Matt Kaufman,** Precicion Metalcraft; **Richard** and **Susan Silvano,** Career Management International; **Glen Sytnyk,** Remax Real Estate; **Sandra Ford,** The Sandra Ford Agency; **Jake Beard** and **Willie Sather,** Morgan Stanley Dean Witter; **John Peterson,** Paine Webber (Jake, Willie, and John being the "Three Wise Men of Wayzata" who have graciously given their approval to the *High Five!* character Jake Sather of Peterson Securities). We also thank **Maxim Worchester** for his understanding and support.

The two teams of support at Ken's and Sheldon's offices, **Dottie Hamilt, Shannon Bajoyo, Eleanor Terndrup, Kelly DeLuca, Kingsley N. Bowles,** and **Rita Loewen** (commonly known as **The Amazing Rita**).

The truly High Five, Gung Ho team that guides our work: **Michael Morrison, Larry Hughes,** and **Michal Yanson** of William Morrow; **Dave Derminio, Dick Lyles,** and **Harry Paul** of The Ken Blanchard Companies, and **Margret McBride,** our literary agent.

We also extend our warmest thanks to **Richard L. Aquan** for designing our magnificent jackets, **Rose-Ann Ferrick** for the superb copyedit and **Nancy Singer Olaguera** for the wonderful design of the book itself. Ultimately, however, the real heroes at Morrow are the salespeople. This High Five team of dedicated individuals is out there, like the postal service, in hail, rain, sleet, and snow, going from store to store, introducing the Morrow list and helping booksellers place orders. It is these men and women, along with the booksellers, who spread the word, and we extend to them our warmest and most sincere thanks.

Last year the Hearst Corporation decided, as Spencer Johnson would say, to move our cheese and sold William Morrow to the fine people at HarperCollins. The relationship between an author and a publisher is more than just a business one. **Jane Friedman,** president and chief executive officer, and **Cathy Hemming,** president and publisher, have been sensitive to our needs and concerns and have given us a warm welcome into the HarperCollins family. We appreciate their doing so and we're honored to be part of the HarperCollins High Five team of talented and dedicated people.

In the fall of 1998 **Margie Blanchard** and **Penny Bowles** were at the meeting Ken and Sheldon held with Don Carew and Eunice Parisi-Carew at which *High Five!* was launched. From that moment on, Margie and Penny have been intimately involved with this project: reading, advising, and editing. We thank them for their love, faith, support, and understanding. Being married to writers, who are apt to be lost in a manuscript or off making a speech when most needed at home, isn't an easy life. We acknowledge the burdens you carry to keep ours light so that we can do what we are called to do. We recognize the often heavy price you must pay to purchase the freedom you lovingly grant us. For this you have all our love and undying gratitude. We also extend our thanks to our children and their spouses: **Debbie** and **Humberto Medina, Scott** and **Chris Blanchard** (whose children **Kurtis** and **Kyle** fill Ken and Margie's hearts with joy and wonder); **Kingsley Bowles** and **Susan Goldie; Patti** and **Kristjan Backman;** and **Aaron Hull**—who really is the smartest tiger in the jungle!

ABOUT THE AUTHORS

KEN BLANCHARD's impact as a writer in the field of management has been far-reaching. *The One Minute Manager* (1982), coauthored with Spencer Johnson, has sold over 9 million copies and has been translated into more than twenty-five languages.

The One Minute Manager plus the trilogy *Raving Fans, Gung Ho!,* and *Big Bucks!* coauthored with Sheldon Bowles, along with *Leadership by the Book* (1999), coauthored with Bill Hybels and Phil Hodges, continue to appear on bestseller lists.

Ken is the Chief Spiritual Officer (CSO) of The Ken Blanchard Companies, a full-service management consulting and training company that he cofounded in 1979 with his wife, Margie. The Blanchards are proud of the fact that their daughter, Debbie, and son, Scott, are also active in their businesses.

The Blanchards are proud grandparents of Kurtis and Kyle, the two wonderful sons of Scott and Chris Blanchard, who live near the Blanchards' hometown of San Diego.

SHELDON BOWLES is a successful entrepreneur, *New York Times* and *Business Week* bestselling author, and noted speaker. He began his career as a newspaper reporter and became vice president of Royal Canadian Securities and then president and CEO of Domo Gas. With partner Douglas Everett, Sheldon built that company into one of Canada's largest retail gasoline chains.

After leaving Domo, Sheldon, with three partners, turned a small manufacturing plant into a multimillion-dollar business. Today, in addition to manufacturing, Sheldon has interests in a recycling and waste-hauling business and is hard at work building the finest full-serve car wash in North America. When not pursuing business opportunities Sheldon shares his hard-won knowledge of what works and what doesn't with audiences around the world and in his books *Raving Fans, Gung Ho!, Big Bucks!* and now *High Five!* all coauthored with Ken Blanchard.

Sheldon, along with his wife, Penny, and their children, Kingsley and Patti, all work together in business and live in Winnipeg, as does the smartest tiger in the jungle—Aaron Hull.

DONALD K. CAREW, a founding member of The Ken Blanchard Companies, is an accomplished and respected author, educator, and organization development consultant who has worked with numerous organizations over the past thirty-five years.

Don has been a faculty member at Trenton State College, Princeton University, Ohio University, the University of San Diego, and the University of Massachusetts at Amherst. At the latter he directed and taught in the graduate program in organization development from 1969 to 1994 and is now a professor emeritus there.

In addition to serving as internal consultant for The Ken Blanchard Companies, he is the coauthor of Blanchard's teamwork products, books, and manuals and of the bestselling book *The One Minute Manager Builds High Performing Teams* with Eunice Parisi-Carew and Ken Blanchard. Donald is a member of NTL Institute and a licensed psychologist in Massachusetts.

EUNICE PARISI-CAREW is a senior researcher with the Office of the Future at The Ken Blanchard Companies. She has extensive management and consultative experience and has taught numerous national and international corporations the importance of maximizing team skills to enhance their businesses.

In addition, Eunice has taught courses in team dynamics and leadership at the University of Massachusetts, the University of Hartford, American University and the University of San Diego. She is a member of NTL Institute and a certified organizational psychologist,

In her role at The Ken Blanchard Companies, Eunice and her colleagues study trends that are likely to impact the world of business three to ten years in the future.

SERVICES AVAILABLE

Ken Blanchard and Sheldon Bowles speak to conventions and organizations all over the world, while Don Carew and Eunice Parisi-Carew train and consult. Blanchard and Bowles's messages are available on audio and video tape.

Extensive training and team-building programs that build on *High Five!* and the PERFORM model are available through The Ken Blanchard Companies. In addition, the companies conduct seminars and in-depth consulting in the areas of teamwork, customer service, leadership, performance management, and quality.

For further information on Ken Blanchard's, Don Carew's and Eunice Parisi-Carew's activities and programs contact:

The Ken Blanchard Companies
125 State Place
Escondido, CA 92025
(800) 728-6000 or (760) 489-5005
(760) 489-8407 (fax)

For further information on Sheldon Bowles's activities and programs contact:

Ode to Joy Limited
5-165 Kennedy Street
Winnipeg R3C 156
Manitoba, Canada
(204) 943-6642
(204) 947-1536 (fax)

On the Web visit:
www.thekenblanchardcompanies.com
www.sheldonbowles.com